PASSING ON THE FAITH:

The Challenge for Parents and Schools

PASSING ON THE FAITH:

The Challenge for Parents and Schools

*Train up a child in the way he should go:
and when he is old, he will not depart from it.* (Proverbs 22.6)

Proceedings of the Christopher Dawson Centre
Colloquium 2021

edited by David Daintree

Christopher Dawson Press
Hobart, Tasmania, Australia
2022

The Christopher Dawson Centre for Cultural Studies
35 Tower Road
New Town
Tasmania 7008
Australia

www.dawsoncentre.org

Copyright © David Daintree 2022

ALL RIGHTS RESERVED. This book contains material protected under International and Federal Copyright Laws and Treaties. Any unauthorised reprint or use of this material is prohibited. No part of this book may be reproduced or transmitted in any form or by any means, electronic or mechanical, including photocopying, recording, or by any information storage and retrieval system without express written permission from the publisher.

ISBN: 978-0-646-85354-3

The editor gratefully acknowledges the generous assistance of Br Gregory Hobbs OSB, of the Notre Dame Priory, Tasmania, for his invaluable contribution to the design and production of this book.

Cover: *Virgin and Child in a niche*,
by Andrea della Robbia, c. 1460
(Public domain by courtesy of the Metropolitan Museum of Art, New York)

CONTENTS

7   **David Daintree**
          Introduction

11   A Summary of Papers

19   **Kenneth Crowther**
          Whose Culture? Which Liberal Arts?

37   **Kevin Donnelly**
          Virtue not Values

45   **Fadi Elbarbar**
          See, Judge, Act: a Lens for Remembering and Living

59   **Gerard Gaskin**
          Catholic Education and the Ascendance of Christian Culture

77   **David Hastie**
          Shifting the Paradigm of initial Teacher Training

105   **Cheryl Lacey**
          Faith and Family: the Fundamental Principles of an Educated Nation

117   **Eamonn Pollard**
          Who are the Adolescents today?

143	**Archbishop Julian Porteous** A Christian Anthropological Creed
155	**Peter Robinson** Governor Bourke's Vision and its current Fruit
179	**Karl Schmude** A University Tradition: Campion and Newman
195	**Wanda Skowronska** Fr Paul Stenhouse vs the 'Gramscian Reset'
211	**Ben and Julianna Smith** Passing on the Faith: Family, Church and School
227	**Robert Van Gend** Tasting the Transcendentals
239	List of the Contributors

PASSING ON THE FAITH: AN OVERVIEW

David Daintree

On behalf of the Christopher Dawson Centre for Cultural Studies, its Patron (Archbishop Porteous), its Committee, and its International Advisory Board, I have pleasure in presenting in one volume the proceedings of our sixth annual Colloquium.

This event, first taking place in 2015, has been the primary object of our striving. We could claim it as an *annual* fixture, were it not for the intervention of Covid and our inevitable cancellation in 2020. But we tried again in 2021, determined to regain our place in the calendar and to stay there, and we managed to assemble a fine programme, in spite of the fact that a few speakers had to attend *in absentia*.

It would be presumptuous for any small organisation such as ours to claim the honourable title of *gadfly*, that Socrates bore, but we shall nevertheless do our best to annoy, irritate or defy purveyors of falsehood masquerading as science, or of bigotry concealed under a pretence of tolerance.

Needless to say, there is much to do.

And the task is getting harder as crazy notions spread like wild fire and become wilder as they spread, often claiming the authority of science, and using the muscle of popular mass culture to cower most people into acquiescence, if not belief. We are indeed in the midst of a pandemic, but it's much bigger than Covid: it's a radical and possibly fatal divergence between reality and imagination. Truth doesn't matter anymore: you are what you think you are, and there's no mercy for the person who tells the emperor that he's naked.

Our focus at this colloquium is on education, and particularly on secondary education, a ground where battles may be fought and lost, battles of such importance that the whole outcome of the greatest of great wars might be decided there.

The proposed new Australian Curriculum has not yet been endorsed by the various state and federal education ministers. Nevertheless the thrust of the document is clearly unsympathetic to the many formative 'Western' strands in our history and culture, and prevailing trends suggest that we are unlikely to see much moderation.

To quantify this, the words *Christian* or *Christianity* occur just seven times in the whole draft document. No less than three of those references are in relation to the history of the Vikings (so they are subsidiary to something else), two couple Christianity with Islam (as if there were not 600 years between the establishment of the two faiths), one links Christianity with the ambitions of the Conquistadors, and the last reports the tolerance of the Ottomans *towards* Christians. *Towards* Christians, mark you! You can't miss the implication that Christians went unprovoked on crusade against peaceful Muslims. One passage discusses the 'triggers of declining Viking power' such as 'changing climate and/or the spread of Christianity'. *Climate change* and *Christianity* – two very great evils in the eyes of the twitterati who are close to dominating our world

By contrast the document mentions the *First Nations* 97 times.

Now it is not the business of this short essay to demean Australia's native peoples. It is entirely right that their story be told. But we are said to be a multicultural and *inclusive* society, which ought to mean, if it means anything at all, that every constituent and contributing cultural group has its own story to tell, and that these stories are all part of the mosaic of modern Australia. Is it unreasonable to say that a ratio of 97:7 suggests a certain imbalance in covering the history of our country?

A curriculum such as this effectively overlooks the *connectedness* of historical events. For example, it is impossible to understand the British and the French without some knowledge of the Greeks and Romans; and it is impossible to understand the situation of indigenous culture without some knowledge of the English, Scots and Irish who played, for better or for worse, a major role in bringing about that fusion that is modern Australia. One example might suffice: the recording and preservation of many of the aboriginal languages that are now sadly extinct, is almost entirely the work of scholars writing in English and using Roman script. And speaking of writing, it was Christian missionaries who took on the task of teaching aboriginal people and sharing with them 'all the wisdom of the Egyptians', in the days before governments interested themselves in mass education.

So it is our task, and has always been our task, even in the face of the most relentless and too often vicious opposition, to impart to our children *the best that has been thought and said* (Matthew Arnold's words) without fear or favour, without regard to partisan calculation, without being bullied by popular notions of political correctness.

Our speakers in this colloquium, this conversation, will diverge on many points but almost certainly concur on the things that matter most. That some things are true and some not. That though none of us in this world will ever fully know Truth we are still obliged to seek it honestly, patiently and tirelessly. That children should be trained up in the way they should go.

A SUMMARY OF THE PAPERS IN THIS BOOK

Kenneth Crowther
Whose Culture, Which Liberal Arts?
If, as Christopher Dawson once wrote, all education is enculturation, a question naturally follows: whose culture? For many convinced of the value of the Liberal Arts, the answer is the culture of Western Civilization. However, as there are numerous ways to approach, understand and engage with Western Civilisation, so are there numerous approaches to understanding Liberal Arts or Classical education. This is, in part, due to the incoherence in contemporary culture when it comes to our metaphysical conception of the world. In this paper, I point toward one of the forgotten ideas that shapes modernity – metaphysical nominalism – and discuss how its hidden impact makes the enculturating educative process frustrating, if not impossible. Based loosely upon Alasdair MacIntyre's work identifying the competing visions of moral discourse in the west, this paper will interrogate the obstacles presented by nominalism in attempting to implement a Liberal Arts approach in a Christian P-12 school.

Kevin Donnelly
Virtues not Values
Iain T. Benson from Australia's Notre Dame University argues using the term values is misleading and dangerous as it is a 'vague term that introduces subjective confusion into moral claims'. Benson goes on to argue "the language of values obscures reality" and its widespread use is being employed 'to drive religion and its moral language to the

margins of culture'. In a secular, supposedly post-Christian age where cultural-left theory prevails employing the language of values undermines Christianity in an attempt to banish it from the public square. In opposition to values Benson mounts a case for what he terms virtues. He argues 'values and virtues are utterly different creatures' on the basis 'Virtues are thick and entailed and have a content and long traditions spanning countries, philosophies and religions: values are thin, unentailed and, well, whatever you want them to be'. School education, especially education involving Christian schools, must reassert the central importance of virtues within an increasingly secular, materialistic age where too many students leave schools morally and spiritually adrift.

Fadi Elbarbar
See, Judge, Act: A Lens for Remembering and Living the Good News.

Religious affiliation is continually declining and responses to this crisis have been almost numberless. This is highlighted by the many submissions to the 2020 Plenary Council. This paper will argue that the best way to introduce (or reintroduce) adolescents to the Church is through social justice, but that social justice without a proper framework may 'feel good' for a time but lacks staying power. 'I just want to make a difference' is an authentic cry from the heart, but how to bring it to fruition? Using the *See, Judge, Act* technique introduced by Cardinal Cardijn (Mater et Magistra: 236), learning about the issue, reflecting theologically, and then acting accordingly, adolescents will 'do' social justice better! This will then naturally lead them into a better understanding and closer relationship with our Lord and His Church.

Gerard Gaskin
Catholic Education and the Ascendance of Christian Culture.
Of all the great social institutions of Christendom, it falls to Catholic education - as an extension of the natural family and the heartland of evangelisation - to be the primordial means of the personal and spiritual formation of the individual. Moreover, Catholic education has been, over the centuries, the driver of a transcendent cultural trajectory towards the ultimate human destiny - union with God. Where Catholic education returns to its biblical roots and acknowledges its immense cultural patrimony it always becomes a leaven in human society. In our post-modern secular world Catholic education needs to recommit to these lofty goals.

David Hastie
Shifting the Paradigm of initial teacher training
This paper will not only argue that challenges face high quality teacher supply into Australian faith-affiliated schools, but that several of these challenges create instability across Australian teacher work-force planning in general, and to understand the former, one must see it as a subset of the latter. The paper then indicates the solution of *Formation in subsidiarity* or *'Training on country, for country'*, and briefly signals that the existing St Phillip's Christian School *Teaching School* model in the NSW Hunter, The Teaching School Alliance Sydney, and the St Thomas Aquinas Teaching School in Tasmania constitute the best future direction for guaranteeing strategic HR stability in Australian Schools in general, and Christian faith-affiliated schools in particular.

Cheryl Lacey
Faith and Family: The Fundamental Principles of an Educated Nation
Education is periodically under the microscope, often under threat, and always under discussion. Debate, however, remains shallow, hiding in the shadows of greed and blame.

This paper will bring to light the danger of accepting these naive views. For decades, all Australian schools have been nurturing the rejection, even deriding of Judeo-Christian values. These circumstances are the consequences of our choices. Whether knowingly, deceitfully or through ignorance, we have all contributed to our present position. To combat this pervasion, the very weapon used by schools must become our nation's saviour. It is not greed and blame. It is the family unit. This is the challenge you'll be expected to accept.

Eamonn Pollard
Who are adolescents today? The case for a holistic formation of the head, heart and hands.
Passing on the Faith to adolescents has always been a challenge and is possibly getting more difficult. By 13 or 14 years old, adolescents are hopefully starting to think critically which often leads to scepticism. The average family now does not pass on the Faith and the average adolescent is often indifferent and can be hostile. Teaching Religious Education in Catholic schools is quite challenging. When looking to develop the faith life of teenagers, we need to start with seeing each individual teenager as a person and not just receptacles to pour faith into. The teenage years are arguably the most difficult in the life cycle. Rates of anxiety, depression and suicide for this age are alarming and getting worse. We need to be clear on the purpose of education generally, Religious Education specifically and Faith-based schools. An experience or experiences of the sacred together with language to express the experience and reflective opportunities are very helpful. This paper will suggest that one way to effectively form teenagers in the Faith is through a mix of formation of the head, heart and hands. Religious Education teachers ideally are people of Faith, with some theological understanding and generally good pedagogical practitioners.

Most Revd Julian Porteous
A Christian Anthropological Creed

Christians are very familiar with the idea of a creed which encapsulates the essential elements of our belief. Creeds distil the faith in summary form and are helpful touchstones for orthodoxy. Social changes are sweeping our culture and significantly altering the way people view the nature of the human person especially in the areas of the nature of marriage, of gender, of sexuality. Most Australians now have an understanding of human nature which conflicts with the Christian understanding, which itself guided Western civilisation for 1500 years. Many in our society are now openly antagonistic towards the Christian understanding of the human person and Christian teaching on certain matters like sexual identity, marriage and respect for. There is a need to clearly articulate a Christian 'anthropological creed', for we cannot seek to educate the human person until we first understand who we are as human beings.

Peter Robinson
How Firm a Foundation? Governor Bourke's vision for Eastern Australia based on common Christianity and its current fruit in state school faith education.

Governor Bourke's vision for public education in Eastern Australia (1832) incorporating General and Special Religious Instruction (1849) was very much of a piece with his determination to enfranchise Catholics and Non-conformists in Eastern Australia, achieved with the Church Act of 1836. His vision for public education supporting and relying on common Christianity through GRI and SRI was at times undermined by the churches in the latter C19th. So why does the legacy of his vision for public education still exist in the three eastern mainland states as well as others? This paper seeks to connect Bourke's seminal contribution to building modern Australia with the continuing operation and development of RE in Australia's state schools where it exists, and to examine what we know about the effectiveness of this form of faith formation and its continuing contribution to the public and religious culture of Australia, including recent political and pedagogical developments which highlight its value in a multi-cultural society.

Ben and Juliana Smith
Seeking the right balance of family, Church and school for passing on the faith

Passing on the faith in a post-Christian culture necessitates a strong and fruitful partnership between the family, the parish and the school. When one or more of these three elements are not functioning well then the overall effectiveness of faith transmission in reduced. This paper will examine the wisdom of the Catholic Church and other Christian writers to establish some benchmarks for this triple play of elements. This framework will then be reviewed in the light of the practical experience of the Smith family whose children have attended systemic Catholic schools, an independent Catholic school, a public school, an independent Christian school and an experience of home schooling during the COVID-19 crisis. The paper will finish by offering a few ideas for future models of Catholic school education in moderately populated areas such as Tasmania.

Karl Schmude
Transmitting a University Tradition: Edmund Campion and John Henry Newman.

Two figures in different eras, the 16th century scholar and martyr, Edmund Campion, and the 19th century theologian and founder of the Oxford Movement, John Henry Newman, shed light on the nature and purpose of university education. This paper explores their insights into the educational purpose of a university, as the crown and completion of formal learning, and the ways in which the university is a cultural channel of spiritual understanding and moral inspiration.

Wanda Skowronska
Guerrilla Resistance in Post-Modernist Times: Fr Stenhouse's Pedagogy

From his earliest years as a priest, Fr Stenhouse's writing had a pedagogical purpose, whether providing Catechetical Supplements for Secondary Schools or in his historically focused books. While Gramscian critique of the Western Christianity was seeping through educational institutions, Fr Stenhouse's clarity was applying cultural 'smelling salts' to them and persistently reminding us all of our extraordinary legacy.

Robert van Gend
Tasting the Transcendentals: Augustine Academy

Young people losing their faith is not altogether new. Why did the young Augustine lose his faith? Why did the Prodigal Son go wayward? Restless young hearts get caught up in the worldly offerings of the big city. Their natural hunger for God and for goodness, beauty and truth, is misdirected to the false food of 'sex, drugs and rock'n'roll'. Just add the constant distraction of social media, and we have a picture of today's prodigal youth. They feel that they're well-fed, but they're actually very sick with the chill of materialism and the bleary vision of relativism. If an undernourished, sandy mix of materialism and relativism is the soil in which young plants grow today, the task of the educator is to convert this soil to realism, to the conviction that there is such a thing as *reality*. In this fertile loam, young plants can put down roots and grow towards the heavens. This paper will compare two education projects, Augustine Academy in Australia and the Pearson Integrated Humanities Institute in Kansas, both involving stargazing, poetry recitations, music and vegetable gardening...

WHOSE CULTURE? WHICH LIBERAL ARTS?

Kenneth Crowther

Christopher Dawson begins his book *The Crisis of Western Education* by recognising that education is enculturation, 'the process by which culture is handed on by the society and acquired by the individual'.[1] However, in Australia today, it is commonly assumed that education is both amoral and a-cultural. Listen to politicians or parents, and education is about facts, skills and job-preparedness, which apparently have nothing to do with morality and have no specific cultural bias. But even if we *were* to grant that education is an enculturating process, we would then be forced to ask, 'Whose culture?' To suggest that education is the transmission of culture from society to individual is to assume there is such a thing as a culture that exists - an interesting proposal in a self-proclaimed multi-cultural, multi-faith, pluralistic society.

One answer to this question is that in the modern West, the appropriate culture is the one we have inherited, that is, Western Civilisation - such is the argument offered by Dawson. But of course, as the roll-out of initiatives from the Ramsay Centre has proven, to many this idea is entirely contestable, if not contemptible. So even if we were to answer our question of 'Whose culture?' with 'the culture established and created by the Liberal Arts,' we would need to stop and recognise that 'Liberal Arts' is now a term meaning just about anything. Today, Liberal Arts includes conducting Marxist readings of Shakespeare proving his

---

[1] Dawson, C. *The Crisis of Western Education*, The Catholic University of America Press, 2010, p.3.

misogynist, patriarchal, capitalist and colonialist inclinations. And thus, the question: 'Whose Culture? Which Liberal Arts?' This title is modelled after Alasdair MacIntyre's, *Whose Justice? Which Rationality?*, in which he traces the historical progress of how rival conceptions of justice and rationality came to coexist within modernity even though they contradict each other, pointing to separate ethical and anthropological conclusions. I believe MacIntyre accurately identifies incoherence at the heart of society, an incoherence that exists also in education. I here intend to point to one specific cause of the cultural incoherence of modernity - metaphysical nominalism - to reveal, and hopefully find a way to navigate around, the obstacles that it creates for education.

Feelings which propel the question at the heart of Christopher Dawson's historical examination of education in the west were also interrogated by T.S. Eliot in the opening stanza to *Choruses from "The Rock"*:

> *The endless cycle of idea and action,*
> *Endless invention, endless experiment,*
> *Brings knowledge of motion, but not of stillness;*
> *Knowledge of speech, but not of silence;*
> *Knowledge of words, and ignorance of the Word.*
> *All our knowledge brings us nearer to our ignorance,*
> *All our ignorance brings us nearer to death,*
> *But nearness to death no nearer to God.*
> *Where is the Life we have lost in living?*
> *Where is the wisdom we have lost in knowledge?*
> *Where is the knowledge we have lost in information?*
> *The cycles of Heaven in twenty centuries*
> *Bring us farther from God and nearer to the Dust.*

Eliot's rendering of these questions suggests a forgetfulness I believe is at the heart of modernity: an anthropological amnesia about who we are. Permit me to provide an illustration of the situation in which we find ourselves. When I was in university studying to become a teacher, I was told that my future students would be 'digital natives'. My professors said that when it came to technology my students would 'know it all,' and it would be second nature to them. But after twelve years of teaching, I can definitively reject this assertion. My students do not know it all. What they know - and know well - is how to use technology. But they do not understand how it works. They know the basics, that 'this button does this'. But that does not mean they know how to troubleshoot when it is not working as expected. To paraphrase Eliot, they have an overabundance of information, some knowledge, very little understanding, and no wisdom.

As a millennial, I am a digital native, because I grew up alongside the digital age, witnessing its progress and evolution. My children, however, are products of a digital age. There is a difference. And it is this same difference between people who have done the work to 'grow up' with modernity, and people who are merely products of modernity. Unlike the digital age, modernity grew up over the course of five hundred years. Therefore, all of us are products of the modern age, but none of us are naturally modern natives, in the sense that I am a digital native. And this presents us with a particular problem: we are a product of something with which we did not grow up and thence do not understand. Of course, there is a way to grow up with modernity, and that is to do the work to understand its birth and development. We do this through studying history which frees us from being blind, aimless, unconscious products of a system of thought, allowing us instead to understand it and therefore to operate as free agents within that age. No individual can have lived from 1300 to 2021 and witnessed firsthand the fullness of modernity's birth and development. But we are all products of this world, products of the process of deconstruction and disenchantment that we so optimistically call modernity. Unfortunately, thanks to the general malignment of real history education in schools, very few people know any of this. We are lost in time, committing the chronological snobbery rebuked by C.S. Lewis.[2] We are adults with no memory of our childhood, and thus, no understanding of who we are. We are so steeped in the cultural milieu, that we cannot see outside of it. Almost by definition to be modern means to not understand what it means to be modern. Thus, we have more questions than answers - though they are questions we do not know to ask, because we cannot even recognise them as possibilities on the horizon of human experience. Therefore 'Whose culture?' or 'Which Liberal Arts?' are questions that remain unasked. Education is about getting a job. There *is* nothing else to talk about, no other question to ask, and if there were, we would lack the capacity to understand the question, let alone start formulating an answer.

This, at least, is my experience. I teach in a Christian school which has recently made the decision to purposefully identify with and locate itself within the Liberal Arts Tradition. The decision to do so is much easier than the actual working out of what that tangibly looks like. This is for many reasons: staff have largely been trained in modern universities and formed to think about education through the confusingly impossible combination of post-structuralism and economic neoliberalism; our students have expectations of school shaped by their experiences and see it as government-legislated drudgery where you sometimes get to play sport; not only do our parents not read classical literature but they read very little of anything and struggle to understand the value of reading in a technological age, deriding Dante and Wordsworth without knowing who they are; the government funding model is tied to what should be taught and when, which is almost fundamentally antithetical to the Liberal Arts; and the list goes on.

All these obstacles stem from our great forgetfulness. Though perhaps forgetfulness is too polite a word,

---

[2] Lewis, C.S., *Surprised by Joy*, HarperOne, 2017, p.206.

considering it is hard to believe that this has not been an intentional amnesia, brought about by the continual concussive barrage of media, ideology and an anti-historical view of history more interested in marginalia than truth. This is more than a forgetting of historical facts or the books and people that made our world. It is an ignorance of the formational moments of modernity, and a determined detestation of everything that came before 'right now'. There are many elements that combined to make the modern world, but today I want to focus on one specific element. And, as with so many seismic shifts in history, it is an idea - not an invention or a revolution or a war - but instead a seemingly irrelevant, complex, and painfully nuanced idea pertaining to a branch of philosophy reserved almost exclusively for academics in ivory towers, yet is inescapably a part of every person's everyday experience: metaphysics.

It all starts with Plato. And perhaps we should not be surprised, for as Professor Diggory Kirke reminds us in C.S. Lewis' *The Last Battle,* 'It's all in Plato, all in Plato.'[3] One of his most famous theories is that of The Forms, a theory which became known as Metaphysical Realism. According to Plato, a concept such as 'Beauty' exists 'in itself'; it is a universal reality in which all things that are in any degree beautiful participate.[4] Aristotle adapted his teacher's idea: not denying the existence of universals, but stating that they were immanent in particulars, rather than existing in and of themselves as Ideal Forms in some transcendent yet actual 'place'. Philosopher Peter Adamson summarises: 'Where Plato thinks of beautiful things as caused by Beauty Itself, Aristotle holds that without beautiful things, there is no such thing as beauty.'[5] Neo-Platonists such as Saint Augustine of

---

[3] Lewis, C.S., *The Last Battle,* Harper Collins, 1980, p.160.
[4] Plato, *Great Dialogues of Plato,* New American Library, 1956, p.276. Plato never wrote a simple and succinct definition of the forms; rather, the theory emerges throughout much of his Socratic Dialogues, primarily the *Meno* and the *Republic.*
[5] Adamson, Peter, *Classical Philosophy* p.213.

Hippo recognised these ideas cohered with the metaphysical claims embedded within Christianity.[6] The Theory of the Forms found root in Christianity by relocating Plato's transcendent realm of ideas into the Divine mind[7] of God, and thus a form of Christian Platonic Realism came to dominate the philosophical and theological landscape for the next thousand years.[8]

Of course, throughout the centuries, these ideas were challenged, adapted, and transformed.[9] The largest of these challenges came from the eleventh century philosopher Peter Abelard, who rejected the medieval realism of his time, stating that universal concepts are merely 'names' - words humans use - and are not ontological entities in and of themselves. Note the translocation from the mind of God to the mind of men. Thus, nominalism was born (*nomen* being Latin for name). Despite this attack on realism, Thomas Aquinas, convinced that 'divine wisdom and valid human reason could not contradict one another'[10] managed to integrate a form of moderate Aristotelean Realism with the pre-existing Christian Platonism and in so doing, held back the power of nominalism for another century or so, that is, until the devastating work of William of Ockham.[11]

---

[6] See Kreeft, Peter, *The Platonic Tradition*.

[7] Klima, Gyula, 'Natures: the problem of universals', in *The Cambridge Companion to Medieval Philosophy*, ed. A.S. McGrade, Cambridge University Press, 2003, p.197.

[8] For a fascinating and compelling discussion of Christian Platonism, see Paul Tyson's *Returning to Reality: Christian Platonism for our Times*. I am much indebted to Dr Tyson for not only this work, but his generous hospitality and conversation around these issues.

[9] Many philosophers, for example, still embraced the hard-lined Platonist perspective that universal forms really did concretely exist in some transcendent place. See Tyson, op. cit., p.72.

[10] Ibid. p.63.

[11] I here join one of three schools of interpretation identified by Heiko Oberman in his introduction to *The Harvest of Medieval Theology*, what he calls the 'Thomistic school of interpretation', which holds that the thought of the period succeeding Aquinas, 'beginning

At the risk of becoming too entrenched in the complexities of this question, which became known as the Problem of Universals, we must discuss the impact that nominalism had on not only modernity, but on Christianity itself. This is due, in part, to Martin Luther's respect for Ockham, as well as his disgust for scholasticism - the philosophical school that harmonised the works of Aristotle and Plato with Christianity.

In his 1525 treatise *The Bondage of Will*, which was a response to Erasmus' *Discussion of Free Will*, Martin Luther praised Erasmus, saying, '[You] have not wearied me with those irrelevant points about popery, purgatory, indulgences and other like baubles ... You, and you alone, saw what was the grand hinge upon which the whole turned, and therefore you attacked the vital part.'[12] It would be surprising for many to hear Luther considering the Papacy, purgatory and indulgences - the very things often assumed central problems - as mere trifles. Instead, he points to a hinge upon which, for him, everything turned. That hinge is scholasticism.[13] Among other reasons, this was due to scholasticism's ready acceptance of Aristotelianism, and Luther vehemently rejected Aristotle's philosophical conceptions of virtue as habit, and happiness as the greatest human end. He believed that these views had infiltrated theology in such a way as to suggest that this virtuous habituation contributed to salvation. In Luther's thinking, scholastic philosophy had become so intertwined with theology that Aristotle's ethics had infected the centrality of grace in the Gospel. This is made clear in his 1517 *Disputation against Scholastic Theology*, in which he unleashes a

---

with Duns Scotus and culminating in nominalism ... is characterized by the disintegration and rapid collapse of the Thomistic synthesis' (I).
[12] Luther, Martin, *On The Bondage of the Will*, 1823 p.376.
[13] While the specific hinge here discussed is the question of free-will and autonomy, it was the scholastic and Aristotelean approach to answering that question which Luther rejected.

series of take-downs on Aristotle and scholasticism, summarised in point 50: 'Briefly, the whole of Aristotle is to theology as darkness is to light. This is in opposition to the scholastics'.[14] This bias against scholasticism meant that Luther, as one of the progenitors of the reforming spirit, was poised to accept other elements of new philosophical approaches, including the new metaphysical approach of William of Ockham, whom he once called 'his dear master'.[15]

Ockham's nominalism was a semantic answer to the Problem of Universals, found entirely in human agency. It is the capacity to think and speak which creates the singular *nomen* which give meaning to singular particulars and order the world so as to *appear* to contain universals. In replacing the 'realist conception of universals with a theory of mental signs,'[16] Ockham rejected not only strict Platonic Realism, but also the more moderate Aristotelean position that statements about the world 'corresponded with the real nature of things as eternally established by God'.[17] While Ockham's answer was a satisfyingly simple alternative to the complex to-and-fro of medieval approaches and revisions of realism, the unintended consequence was that the removal of universals as existing eternally in the mind of God resulted in disconnecting God from the world.[18] The continued impact on theology was profound. As Andrew Wright summarises:

> *William of Ockham dismissed the received scholastic synthesis of faith and reason on the grounds that any attempt, however limited, to make*

---

[14] Luther, Martin, *Career of the Reformer,* Fortress Press, 1957, p.12.
[15] Luther, Martin, *Exhortation to All Clergy Assembled at Augsburg.*
[16] Hudson, Nicholas, 'John Locke and the Tradition of Nominalism', in, *Nominalism and Literary Discourse New Perspectives*, Ed. Hugo Keiper, Christopher Bode and Richard J. Utz, Rodopi, 1997, p.285
[17] Ibid.
[18] This disconnecting process was assisted by other well-intended ideas, including Duns Scotus' Univocity of Being. Tyson, op. cit. p.64.

God accountable to human reason risked compromising divine sovereignty. His nominalist distinction between the reality of particulars and non-reality of universals effectively drove a wedge between the historical Jesus and the Christ of faith. Though this enabled him to assert the absolute transcendence, otherness and freedom of God, it also denied theological discourse any secure purchase on reality.[19]

Nominalism continued to gather a strong following, and by the seventeenth and eighteenth centuries:

The term 'nominalism' itself fell from ordinary usage, and the great controversy between nominalists and realists receded into history ... But nominalism had mutated into radically new forms. William of Ockham himself would been shocked to discover what strange and heretical doctrines had evolved from his first principles.[20]

By the Twentieth Century, the Swiss theologian Hans Urs von Balthasar could reflect upon nominalism as a major source of the secularism that infected Western culture and deprived the world of meaning. 'A kind of testing of metaphysical love came with the epochal darkening of the fourteenth century,' he writes, and in response, 'philosophers strain and storm nominalistically and shatter the web of the world dialectically'.[21] Balthasar points to the likes of Francis Bacon, Thomas Hobbes and John Locke, as major proponents of nominalism in varying degrees of extremity.[22] Before long, nominalism had become even the denial of that which it itself originally posited. Locke, for example, 'rejected not only realism, but also Ockham's nominalistic doctrine that universal concepts were "natural"

---

[19] Wright, Andrew, *Religious Education and Critical Realism: Knowledge, Reality and Religious Literacy*, p.5.
[20] Hudson, op.cit. p.283.
[21] Von Balthasar, Hans, Urs, *The Glory of the Lord: Volume 5*, Ignatius, 1991, p.641.
[22] Von Balthasar, Hans, Urs, *The Glory of the Lord: Volume 5*, Ignatius, 1991, p.289.

signs' at all.[23] In other words, names ascribed to reality are an entirely abstracted language, not a response to real nature, because there either is no real nature to know, or real nature is entirely unknowable. While perhaps the earliest iterations of nominalism were largely harmless, through its continued reconfigurations in the hands of enlightenment philosophers, it became a powerfully destructive tool.

Here we return to 2021, a world shaped by this desecrating force, but whose population has no knowledge of its existence or of any alternatives. To refer again to my co-opting of MacIntyre's argument, there exist today, with seeming harmony, rival conceptions of metaphysics, and by extension, education. However, people do not recognise that conceptions other than their own: a) exist, b) are valid, or c) are incompatible with theirs. The harmony, however, is dependent upon the discourse predominating the public sphere. Why was sensible debate around the question of same-sex marriage so hard to come by? Why do we struggle to have non-emotive rational discussion about issues such as abortion, gender, or race? Because it is in these discussions that our rival conceptions rear their otherwise-invisible heads. It is here that unconscious metaphysical assumptions that usually lay dormant on the seabed of subjectivity awaken from their slumber to throw confusion and inarticulate rage into the mix. This confusion is not merely *between* sub-cultures: it is not as if there is a united front amongst secular humanists regarding gender theory, and a united front within Christendom opposing them. No, this confusion is *within* these sub-cultures. The powerful metaphysical overhaul of nominalism which ultimately contributed significantly to the growing secularisation of society through its continued revisiting, remodelling and repurposing by increasingly secular philosophers is not restricted to secular atheist society. Nominalism is everywhere, in everything: not only Protestants, but Catholics and Orthodox, Jews and Muslims

---

[23] Hudson, op. cit. p.285.

are all products of modernity, and as such, all have nominalism flowing through their veins, even if they do not know what it is.

Hopefully now we might begin to see the obstacles that are presented to the modern educator who takes seriously the truth that education is enculturation, and the proposal that Liberal Arts is the best way to do so. If, as nominalism suggests, there is no intrinsic meaning in the world, education *cannot* be about anything other than pragmatic skill-attainment. It cannot be what John Ruskin sees as the purpose of true education: 'To make people not merely do the right things, but enjoy the right things - not merely industrious, but to love industry - not merely learned, but to love knowledge - not merely pure, but to love purity - not merely just, but to hunger and thirst after justice'.[24] Ruskin's sentiment here aligns to that established in Lewis' *The Abolition of Man*, which identifies the Platonic and Augustinian concept of *ordo amoris* as the purpose of education.[25] For there to be an ordered love - for there to exist right and wrong responses to the world - the things in the world must be real ontological entities that exist apart from our definition of them. Waterfalls must really *be* sublime, rather than 'sublime' being merely a word to express the feelings of a subject viewing some inert, neutral, mechanistic natural phenomena.[26]

While many educators and parents, particularly those identifying as Christians, may accept the ideas of Lewis and Ruskin when they remain in the comfortable realms of broadly accepted ethics, the rebellion and dissonance begins when this realism encroaches upon their personal desires. Everyone is okay with teaching students justice. In the Australian National Curriculum it is included as a 'General Capability', as well as in both Civics and Citizenship and

---

[24] Ruskin, *The Crown of Wild Olive*, Colonial Press Company, 2008, p.46.
[25] Lewis, C.S., *The Abolition of Man*, HarperOne, 2001, p.16.
[26] Ibid. p.2.

Health and Physical Education courses. However, as MacIntyre would ask, whose justice? What definition of justice?[27] In a nominalist world, justice is only a *nomen*, a name, merely semantics defined by the individual, and thus all teaching becomes relativised. We cannot engage in the passing of a culture from one to another, because the culture of nominalism rejects the existence of a culture at all. There are only subjects, and only subjectivism. A teacher is not a part of a larger cultural organism passing that culture to the next generation. A teacher is only a singular individual in a sea of individuals, disconnected.

Of course, while this may be the logical outcome of nominalism, it does not align with our day-to-day lived experience. Operating functionally in a purely subjectivised and relativised world is impossible. As Paul Tyson remarks, 'I cannot see that it would actually be possible to relate to real people and be an actor in the real world without assuming that reality had qualitative and meaningful dimensions'.[28] Despite our straining against them, there remain immutable realities. This is seen clearly in the fact that while on the meta-scale political talk around education is economic, it very quickly becomes ideological and decidedly realist when it wants to. The most recent example of this is perhaps the need for schools to teach about consent[29] - not the nature of humanity, the meaning of sexual union, or even the mere biological purpose of the sexual act. We cannot teach about these things, because

---

[27] For example, the context of ACARA's Health and Physical Education is as follows: 'The HPE curriculum supports critical inquiry where students analyse the factors that influence decision-making, behaviours and actions and explore inclusiveness, power inequalities, assumptions and social justice.'

[28] Tyson, Paul, op. cit. p.19.

[29] I am not here suggesting that consent education should not necessarily take place in schools, but merely using it as an example of the disconnected nature of the educational process. It also strikes me as an unfortunate example of schools filling the void left by other long-standing institutions such as the church and family.

according to nominalism, they do not actually exist. All that exists is the Nietzschean conception of will, and therefore, all that be spoken of is consent. But what is will, if not a metaphysical reality? There is always *something* that needs to be treated as a universal.

However the very fact that government attempts to legislate the teaching of ideas such as consent or gender theory suggests that when thinking along those lines, these institutions are not nominalists.[30] The fact that this stuff *should* be taught, rests upon a non-relativist, non-nominalist metaphysical platform, because claims of *should* or *ought* belong to realism, whereas claims like, 'You make your own decisions and it's up to you,' stem from nominalism. This is the incoherence and confusion which modern education has become, and into which it is enculturating the next generation. If nothing else, education should be coherent. We should not be enculturating young people into a culture in which nothing makes sense, in which there is no logical continuity, in which 2+2=5.

This means that even though a Christian School in the Liberal Arts Tradition may not fall into some of nominalism's more obvious snares, it is still populated by students, teachers and families who have been shaped by it. The sixteenth century reformers accepted nominalism as a foundational element of protestant theology, contributing to the secularising of the West into which we are all born. If

---

[30] This is even though a theory of gender in which gender is 'nothing but a name' would be possibly one of the clearest examples of nominalism in action in today's age. The feminist philosopher Linda Alcoff identified this in her 1988 article, 'Cultural Feminism versus Post-Structuralism: The Identity Crisis in Feminist Theory', in the journal *Signs* (3:13), when she wrote that 'a feminist adoption of nominalism ... threatens to wipe out feminism itself'. In discussing Biddy Martin's work, she writes, 'What is a woman? If the category "woman" is fundamentally un- decidable, then we can offer no positive conception of it that is immune to deconstruction, and we are left with a feminism that can be only deconstructive and, thus, nominalist once again' (420).

unsure of the extent of its impact, perhaps we could look to our students' spiritual health as an indication. Roger Scruton, commenting on what he calls the 'metaphysical loneliness' in every human, talks of the metaphysical 'sacramental bond that is established when people adopt common myths, common liturgies, and a common distinction between the sacred and the profane'.[31] No wonder, in a world shaped by shapelessness, in which the naturally membership-bestowing processes of enculturation such as family and church have been eroded, schools are seen as the last bastion of identity-formation. But in nominalism there are no common myths, common liturgies, or commonly held sanctity, and schools can at best offer incoherent subjectivism which students subconsciously recognise as empty, and our metaphysical loneliness threatens to overwhelm. As R.J. Snell explains, citing Charles Taylor:

> *Modern freedom resulted when older moral horizons were uprooted, when "liberation" from the "captivity" of divine order was attained. Free, yes, but the world seems to have lost its story, and we suffer "a sense of malaise, emptiness." As Taylor explains in* A Secular Age, *our freedom is disembedded from reality, with a resulting "terrible flatness in the everyday," the "utter flatness, emptiness of the ordinary." Our freedom came at a cost: the loss of anything worth living for, and the only remainder is a "centring on the self." And since the world is devoid of thickness, everything becomes a plaything, something to tame, toy with, lead about on a leash, and discard when we have drained its temporary pleasure.*[32]

Here we must reflect that simply 'teaching the Liberal Arts' is not a remedy for this centring on the self. The Liberal Arts are not immune. It was, after all, wise men of the past trained specifically in the Liberal Arts who not only invented nominalism but continued to warp it and unleash its

---

[31] Scruton, Roger, *Philosophy: Principles and Problems*, Bloomsbury, 2016, p.58.
[32] Snell, R.J. *Acedia and Its Discontents*, pubclish and page

destructive power upon the world. And so we ask, 'which Liberal Arts?' The remedy will not be the Liberal Arts of the modern progressive Left, in which 'liberal' no longer means the liberating power of truth and wisdom, but rather the promise of a freedom to do and be whatever one desires, a liberation from the weight of meaning through deconstructionism. It will not be the attempt at an amoral Liberal Arts hoping to de-westernise the canon, for there is nothing amoral about an ideology that rejects some biases in favour of others. It needs, therefore, to be more than just 'Liberal Arts'. Even the Liberal Arts promoted by Cardinal John Henry Newman, who so wisely recognised that, 'Though the useful is not always good, the good is always useful'[33] will fall afoul of nominalism until we accept that the good is a transcendental reality, and not a subjectively determined word existing only in our own minds.

Teaching within the nominalist tradition means not teaching any tradition at all. Nominalism, however, does not empty the world of meaning, because the world is intrinsically meaningful. All it can do is blind us to that meaning, convincing us we can pick and choose. It cannot be coherent, it can never be consistent, and thus it will always be confusing. Can a culture be passed on, as Dawson suggests, when that culture does not even know if it exists, if that culture cannot identify even itself, and if that culture is completely unaware of *why* it does not know itself? It cannot. For education to be what it really is, a school attempting to regain the lost *telos* of the institutionalised educational act must not only reject nominalism, but must take its teachers, students and wider community on the journey of understanding nominalism. This has been, and continues to be, my experience. This is the reason I can be discussing ideas with fellow teachers, and suddenly someone disagrees with a point that logically follows from all the points with which they have hitherto agreed, because

---

[33] Newman, John, Henry, *The Idea of A University*, Aerterna Press, 2015, p.117.

suddenly their deeply-held nominalism rears its head to rebel against an encroachment upon something they hold dear. Nominalism is, I suggest, a first thing. It is part of a metaphysical platform upon which all other understanding is built. How can education really take place, how can knowledge, understanding, wisdom and culture be passed from master to pupil, if ultimately there is nothing real to pass on? Masters, in fact, could not even exist, which is potentially one of the reasons behind the recent fad of student-centred learning.[34] Nominalism empties out; it attempts to place humanity on the throne of meaning-making, giving us the illusion of being the great definers of reality, but in doing so, it sacrifices the meaning of that reality upon the altar of freedom.[35] If education does not grapple with and reject nominalism, it can do nothing better than forge little pretend gods who grow up to believe they can bend reality to their will, but against whom reality will ultimately win.

Another of T.S. Eliot's despairing reflections upon modernity, written before his turn to Christianity, is *The Hollow Men*. It opens:

> *We are the hollow men*
> *We are the stuffed men*
> *Leaning together*
> *Headpiece filled with straw. Alas!*
> *Our dried voices, when*
> *We whisper together*
> *Are quiet and meaningless*
> *As wind in dry grass*

---

[34] In contrast to C.S. Lewis' reflection in *Our English Syllabus*, 'You see at once that it implies an immense superiority on the part of the teacher ... In education, the master is the agent, the pupil, the patient'. pp.83-84.
[35] So much more is said on this important topic in *Acedia and its Discontents*, by RJ Snell.

> *Or rats' feet over broken glass*
> *In our dry cellar*
> *Shape without form, shade without colour,*
> *Paralysed force, gesture without motion…*

This is an image of a world emptied out by nominalism, in which humanity is empty, yet stuffed; where shapes have no form, shades have no colour, force is paralysed, and gesture is motionless. Whose culture? Which Liberal arts? Whichever it is that lights a candle in the darkness and distortion of modernity and rejects the hollowing-out of nominalism. A Christian School in the Liberal Arts Tradition must do the work to 'grow up' with modernity, taking their teachers and students on the journey with them. Until we return to embracing the weight and density of reality, and at the same time the necessary, beautiful and life-giving limitations it imposes upon us, truly enculturing education will be empty, incoherent and meaningless; it will, in fact, be impossible.

VIRTUES NOT VALUES

Kevin Donnelly AM

The following draws on Iain Benson's contribution to the 2017 colloquium titled 'Values Language: A Cuckoo's Egg or Useful Moral Framework?'[1] and a UK publication titled *Rethinking Christian Ethos* by David Albert Jones and Stephen Barrie.[2]

In 2005 the then Prime Minister John Howard sparked a debate about the place of values in schools when arguing the reason so many parents were choosing non-government schools was because government schools were too 'too politically correct and values neutral'.[3] I'd suggest while the first part of the statement is credible the second part ignores the reality every approach to education involves a particular value judgment regarding the purpose of education and what it means to be educated.

In response to the Prime Minister's observation the commonwealth department of education was asked to

---

[1] Iain Benson. 'Values Language: A Cuckoo's Egg or Useful Moral Framework?', in David Daintree (ed), *Creative Subversion: The Liberal Arts and Human Education al Fulfilment* (Hobart/Tas: Connor Court Publishing, 2018) 1-43.

[2] David Albert Jones & Stephen Barrie. *Thinking Christian Ethos* (London/England, 2015).

[3] The Age. 'PM queries the value of state schools'. https://www.theage.com.au/national/pm-queries-values-of-state-schools-20040120-gdx5ac.html Accessed 29 July 2021

develop and make available to schools material related to how best to teach values. The project was titled the National Framework for Values in Australian Schools and values education was defined as:

> *Any explicit and/or implicit school-based activity which promotes student understanding and knowledge of values, and which develops the skills and dispositions of students so they can enact particular values as individuals and as members of the wider community.*[4]

The values listed Australian schools, both government and non-government, were asked to teach included:

1. Care and compassion.
2. Doing your best.
3. Fair go.
4. Freedom.
5. Honesty and trustworthiness.
6. Integrity.
7. Respect.
8. Responsibility.
9. Understanding, tolerance and inclusion.[5]

Fast forward to today's Australian national curriculum and values education is still considered an important part of the school curriculum. One of the 7 general capabilities informing the foundation to year 10 curriculum and applicable to all subject areas is described as 'ethical

---

[4] Commonwealth Department of Education, Employment and Workplace Relations. 'About Values Education',
http://www.curriculum.edu.au/values/val_about_values_education, 8679.html Accessed 21 July 2021.
[5] Commonwealth Department of Education, Employment and Workplace Relations. *National Framework for Values in Australian Schools* (Canberra 2005).
http://www.curriculum.edu.au/verve/_resources/framework_pdf_version_for_the_web.pdf Accessed 22 July 2021.

understanding'. In a statement to teachers explaining what is meant by ethical understanding reference is made to values. The statement reads:

Ethical understanding involves students building a strong personal and socially oriented ethical outlook that helps them to manage context, conflict and uncertainty, and to develop an awareness of the influence their values and behaviour have on others.[6]

The ethical values listed include: 'honesty, resilience, empathy and respect for others and the capacity to act with ethical integrity'. If students are to act ethically teachers are also told they must 'take account of ethical considerations such as human rights and responsibilities, animal rights, environmental issues and global justice'.[7]

In 1946 George Orwell in *Politics and the English Language* wrote: 'Modern English, especially written English, is full of bad habits'.[8] The two examples of teaching values in schools previously referred to illustrate how the problem of vague and imprecise language is still with us.

Listing values like 'Doing your best', 'Fair go' and 'Respect' does nothing to explain why such values are important or, more importantly, detail on what basis such values should be considered preferable and worthwhile. Stating that students need to build 'a strong personal and socially oriented ethical outlook', once again, fails to provide teachers and students with a clear and succinct explanation of what particular belief system or philosophy underpins such a value.

---

[6] Australian Curriculum, Assessment and Reporting Authority. Australian National Curriculum. *Ethical Understanding* https://www.australiancurriculum.edu.au/f-10-curriculum/general-capabilities/ethical-understanding/ Accessed 21 July 2021.
[7] Ibid. Accessed 22 July 2021.
[8] George Orwell. *Politics and the English Language.* https://www.orwellfoundation.com/the-orwell-foundation/orwell/essays-and-other-works/politics-and-the-english-language/ Accessed 21 July 2021

Similarly, while making specific mention of 'human rights and responsibilities, animal rights, environmental issues and global justice' will address the concerns held by woke activists it also fails to detail and justify why such behaviour is preferable.

In addition, such motherhood statements do nothing to help teachers understand what needs to be done in terms of the curriculum and what happens in the classroom.

Even worse, telling students to 'respect another person's point of view' and to 'be aware of others and their cultures' and 'accept diversity' is in danger of leading to moral relativism. Not all points of view are valid or sound and there are some cultural practices that are uncivilised and unacceptable. Respecting multiculturalism should not mean accepting the mistreatment of homosexuals in theocratic countries where fundamentalist Islam prevails. Similarly, the Hindu caste system where individuals are ranked according to birth is unacceptable regardless of the call to accept cultural diversity and difference. Respecting others and being inclusive should never mean tolerating the intolerable.

In opposition to referring to values when deciding how one should live one's life and relate to others and the wider world Iain Benson refers to virtues. Benson argues using the term 'values' is misleading and dangerous as it constitutes a 'vague term that introduces subjective confusion into moral claims'.[9] Benson goes on to argue 'the language of values obscures morality'[10] and its widespread use is being employed to 'drive religion and its moral language to the margins of culture'.[11] Based on the need for education to provide a unifying common ground without which societies fragment Benson also makes the point 'Virtues entail and always have, a shared moral tradition, values do not despite some simply asserting they do'.[12]

---

[9] Iain Benson. Op Cit. 3
[10] Iain Benson. Op Cit. 6
[11] Iain Benson. Op Cit. 8
[12] Iain Benson. Op Cit. 6

In opposition to values one of the primary aims of school education should be to instil virtues. Especially in an increasingly materialistic and narcissistic age it's vital young people are morally and ethically grounded. Given the high rates of youth depression and suicide, the pervasive, alienating influence of social networking sites and accessibility of dehumanising pornography virtues are also critically important.

While the Australian national curriculum defines the purpose of education in terms of 21st century skills, respecting diversity and difference (the new code for multiculturalism) and saving the planet it's time to emphasise a more profound, enriching and lasting sense of what it means to be educated.

A technocratic view of education emphasising skills, in particular, fails to adequately address the central question of how best to decide what constitutes right and wrong action and how best to contribute to the common good.

It's also time to reject education being defined in terms of neo-Marxist inspired politically correct ideology and group think. A godless view of education antithetical to virtues that can be traced to the Italian Marxist Antonio Gramsci and his concept of cultural hegemony. Gramsci argues one of the principal ways capitalist societies reproduce themselves is by indoctrinating citizens via the education system and that if revolutionaries are to succeed they must win control of schools and universities.

Linked with cultural hegemony is Louis Althusser's concept of the ideological state apparatus. Althusser argues capitalism reproduces itself by either using physical violence and intimidation, described as the repressive state apparatus, and/or by conditioning citizens through society's institutions, including the education system.

Michael Liccione describes 1968 as 'one of the most significant years of the twentieth century, at least in the

Western world'.¹³ This was a time when students rebelled and took to the streets in Paris, thousands marched around the world in protest against America's involvement in the Vietnam War and radical feminists and gay/lesbian activists sought liberation from an unjust and oppressive, heteronormative society.

The cultural revolution of the late 60s and early 70s also led to the re-emergence of neo-Marxist critical theory associated with the Frankfurt School established in Germany during the 1920s and the emergence of a rainbow alliance of theories ranging from postmodernism, deconstructionism to radical gender, queer and postcolonial tropes and narratives. While often in disagreement, what all such theories have in common is opposition to a spiritual and transcendent view of the world and the concept of virtues as classically understood.

Similar to Benson and in opposition to a utilitarian, superficial and ideologically driven approach that prioritises values Jones and Barrie in *Thinking Christian Ethos* define education, by necessity, as involving virtues. They write the purpose of education involves:

> ... *the integral formation of the human person, through the cultivation of moral and intellectual virtues, for the good of the person and for the common good of society.*¹⁴

The belief that virtues are central to promoting human flourishing, deciding how best to live one's life and what constitutes the common good has been argued since the time of Plato, Aristotle, Augustine and Aquinas. Such virtues range from truthfulness, magnanimity, prudence, justice, fortitude and temperance to what Aquinas refers to as 'faith, hope and love'.

---

[13] Michael Liccione. 'Ratzinger and del Noce on 1968 and Beyond' in Eds, Thomas V. Gourlay and Daniel Matthys, *1968: Culture and Counterculture*, (USA: Pickwick Publications, 2020) 236-252

[14] David Albert Jones & Stephen Barrie. Op Cit. 53.

Such virtues, whether argued from a secular or Christian perspective, also underpin and shape the concept of a liberal education dedicated to the formation of character. As argued by TS Eliot the purpose of education, in its fullest sense, involves the pursuit of truth, humility and, where possible, the attainment of wisdom.[15] In literature, for example, beginning with Aesop's Fables and classical fairy tales and moving on to Greek tragedies, the works of Shakespeare and modern authors including Charles Dickens, Jane Austen, Mark Twain, Ibsen, Dostoyevsky, Graham Greene, C S Lewis and Patrick White, to name a few, students encounter significant moral and ethical questions associated with the various virtues. Studying history including epochal events like the French Revolution, the American War of Independence and more recently the rise of fascism and communism also centre on what constitutes right and wrong action and how best to contribute to a more just world where people and governments are motivated by truthfulness and magnanimity.

Schools, both faith-based and secular, have a unique and vital role to play in teaching virtues; both in terms of how schools are managed, staffed, and when deciding the curriculum and what occurs in the classroom. In an increasingly materialistic and ego-driven world virtues provide an enduring and compelling framework when determining what constitutes right and wrong action and how best to find personal fulfilment and best to contribute to society.

Virtues such as courage, faith, hope and temperance are especially needed at a time when so many young people are adversely affected by cyber bullying and the widespread availability of pornography made possible by the new forms of digital technology.

At a time when neo-Marxist inspired cultural-left ideology has taken the long march and infiltrated schools it is also

---

[15] See TS Eliot. *Notes Towards a Definition of Culture.* (London: Faber and Faber, 1954) 123

vital to re-establish the necessity of acting morally and ethically. A view that draws on a liberal view of education and the necessity to cultivate what Jones and Barrie describe as 'those dispositions of character conducive to fostering friendship and human flourishing: human moral excellences or virtues'.[16]

---

[16] David Albert Jones & Stephen Barrie. Op Cit, 27.

SEE, JUDGE, ACT: A LENS FOR REMEMBERING AND LIVING THE GOOD NEWS

Fadi Elbarbar

In line with my own teaching practice, stories are necessary to contextualise the lesson, and to bring the reader into the 'behind-the-scenes' of the importance of the lesson. I feel the need to preface my paper with two stories that bookend my experience that has led me to write this paper. The first is how I came to learn about the See, Judge, Act (SJA) process, which in turn brought me to Catholicism, and the second validated that choice with unmatched clarity. Both experiences are also very relevant for how the SJA process can bring people to the faith, and the danger of not having a faith.

In 2009, during my first year of teaching, a student leader came into my Year 9 class and politely asked if he could interrupt to make an announcement. He wanted to remind the class that there was a sausage sizzle fundraiser this week for 'East Africa'. A young boy in my class raised his hand and asked him what he meant, or more accurately, where exactly the money raised would be going. The response? 'Just shut up and buy a sausage'! I was stunned. Not by the language, but by the lack of knowledge. How could a teacher send a student around with this message and not have spoken to them about the cause they were raising for? I delved into this deeply, completing a social justice course with Caritas Australia that year and beginning what would turn into a very strong, very large, and very successful social justice group where I can confidently say that students knew the issues they were raising funds, raising awareness, and advocating for. It was in this process, that I also fall in love with Catholic Schools, and Catholicism – I participated in the RCIA process in 2015. The Catholic School is mandated by its call to follow in the footsteps of our Saviour to 'do' social justice, and 'do' it well. This is what led me to the faith, having previously been loosely affiliated through my family with the Greek Orthodox tradition. The purpose of this paper, is to look at how this can happen for secondary students, using the same method that hooked me in.

Fast forward to 2020, and my best friend, the Godfather of my youngest son, no less, is one of many who have lost their way. Affiliating himself with the infamous QAnon movement and believing every conspiracy theory that you can dream up, he says he is happy, and his life is brimming with positive affirmations, healing through the power of numerology and hypnotherapy, and most recently, the consumption of magic mushrooms, that has harmed and ruined many of his relationships. It became quite clear to me in my discussions with him that my faith, being grounded in something that is cemented in millennia of tradition and having a process that helps me discern what I am going through and what is happening around me, helped me cope with the disruption 2020 threw at me. In the year where my friend who does not have a faith to fall back on, fall apart, I experienced my best professional, personal, physical, and spiritual year of my life to date. The difference was staggering, and I have my faith, and the SJA process, that I have come to use in my everyday life, to thank for this.

I encourage the use of the SJA process, therefore, with these two stories in my mind. The process will help students understand the beautiful and rich tradition of the Church and encourage them to turn to it in times of discernment. It will also give them a foundation to stand confidently on in times of crisis and help them think critically before falling into the increasingly complex and malicious traps presented to them in today's world. Both are interconnected and equally critical.

See, Judge, Act: Definition and History

'Between the first step, which is to come close and allow yourself to be struck by what you see, and the third step, which is to act concretely to heal and repair, there is an essential intermediate stage: to discern, and to choose. A time of trial is always a time of distinguishing the paths of the good that lead to the future from other paths that lead nowhere or backwards. With clarity, we can better choose the first'.

Pope Francis in *Let us Dream: The Path to a Better Future*[1].

The *See, Judge, Act* process is designed to respond to the 'Signs of the Times'. A way of dealing with current issues. There are many ways to define the process, and this is a simplified version for the purpose of this paper:

See: Learning about the issue. Looking at the facts, listening to stories of those affected, hearing both sides of the story. See is also about looking at the lens by which we are seeing the issue and questioning this lens. All in all, the aim of see is to get a complete picture of a situation.

Judge: Reflecting on the issue. Looking at the reasons why the issue being discussed has occurred or continues to occur. This section focuses on looking at the root causes of the issue from different perspectives, such as the social, historical, economic, environmental and political. This part is also about reflecting theologically on this issue, namely, what has the Church said in the past about this issue, or what would Jesus do if he was here now? This involves looking

---

[1] Pope Francis, 2020.

at scripture passages, discussing biblical values, and looking to Catholic Social Teaching.

Act: Acting based on these steps. What actions are appropriate based on the first two steps? The action here needs to be holistic and inclusive. Fundraising, awareness raising, advocacy, and actions of solidarity are all important here. The actions should aim to transform the social structures that contribute to the issue.

The process is also cyclical, once an action has been completed, it is important to think about what other issues arose that need to be discussed and acted on, for example.

The *See, Judge, Act* Process, was first coined and used by Belgian Catholic priest Joseph Cardijn. Cardijn was the founder of the Young Christian Workers (YCW) in 1924, an organisation that was created to give laypeople an opportunity to discuss and discern issues they were seeing[2]. 'Cardijn introduced the process of seeing, judging, and acting in meetings of the YCW to encourage people to observe situations, to evaluate them based on the Gospels, and to act in ways that respond to observed injustices'[3]. The method was solidified as church teaching in Pope John XXIII's encyclical on Christianity and Social Progress, Mater et Magistra[4]:

There are three stages which should normally be followed in the reduction of social principles into practice. First, one reviews the concrete situation; secondly, one forms a judgment on it in the light of these same principles; thirdly, one decides what in the circumstances can and should be done to implement these principles. These are the three stages that are usually expressed in the three terms: look, judge, act.

---

[2] Wilke, 1984, p. 253.
[3] Brigham, 2019.
[4] Pope John XXIII, 1961.

See

As Dr David Daintree explained in his call for papers of which this is one, 'The Christian Church is in decline in Western countries, especially and most tragically among the young'[5]. Bishop Robert Barron, whose work in the area of evangelising to the 'nones', has become his brand[6], says 'After the sex abuse scandal, the massive attrition of the young is, I think, the most important issue facing the Church'[7]. This is the issue we are dealing with, the problem which I hope to contribute some thought to in this paper. In this part, we will attempt to see, hear and experience the lived reality of our youth, and examine the primary data of the situation.

Let's begin where most data analysis does, with the Australian Census. The most recent data available to us reveals that between 2011 and 2016 alone, Christianity declined by 7% at the same time 'No Religion' increased by 48%[8]. This is worrying; almost one in three people declare themselves to have no religion. There have been many explanations offered in regard to this alarming statistic, including how the question is asked in the census[9], and the way in which responses are categorised[10], for example. However, we cannot get caught in this argument, because we who have an interest in religious affiliation, see it ourselves every day. The number may not be accurate to the percentage point, but it is close – and that is where our concern must focus. The number is greater in those aged 34 and under. 34.2% of those under 18, and 38.7% of those between 18 and 34, declare to have no religion[11]. There are

---

[5] Daintree, 2021.
[6] Clemmer, 2019.
[7] Barron, 2019.
[8] Australian Bureau of Statistics, 2017.
[9] Jensen, 2020.
[10] Tau and Stapleton, 2020.
[11] Australian Bureau of Statistics, 2017.

many other ways of unpacking this data, such as The National Centre for Pastoral Research, and their Social Profile of the Catholic Community in Australia 2016 Report, or the work of the National Church Life Survey. The number of 'nones' is the focus here, however.

In Australia, a process of discernment has already commenced that can help us understand why people are turning away from the Church. The Plenary Council released its first report in 2019. *Listen to what the Spirit is Saying: Final Report for the Plenary Council Phase I: Listening and Dialogue*[12], and it provides many insights into this question of declining religious affiliation. Mass being unappealing for youth and children (pp. 51-52), the need to reach out explicitly to youth (pp. 124-125), and the need for a better interface between parish and school (p. 163), stand out as three examples cited in this report. There is also a whole section dedicated to Youth Ministry (pp. 142-147), which includes the need to better train youth leaders, which in turn can lead to better youth faith formation, and provide more youth facilities and programs, in order to attract and retain young people. However, the report is peppered with many other 'areas of improvement' which can all be used as reasons for the decline of religious affiliation. Priests who do not understand the Australian context, or are 'out of touch', the sexual abuse scandal that has decimated the Church globally, the role of women in the Church, are all issues students understand, are aware of, or at the very least, does little to help a parent encouraging their child to attend mass or learn more about their faith.

Being interviewed for his book, *Beyond Belief: How we find meaning, with or without religion*[13], Hugh Mackay explains that people are turning their back on religion because it contradicts the message being pushed by mass marketing 'where we are told life's greatest satisfaction is to 'buy, buy, buy", because the Church is 'a big, global corporation … [it

---

[12] Dantis, Bowell, Reid and Dudfield, 2019.
[13] Mackay, 2019.

is] not very welcoming ... the experience is seen as boring and quite irrelevant', and 'we have the dogmatic association with religion: to be Christian, you have to believe that miracles have happened'. All three relate to the points mentioned in the reflection on the Plenary Council report and relate to something Bishop Barron focuses on in his work on the issue of the 'nones'. One of the reasons Bishop Barron gives for the attrition of the young is the lack of understanding of the faith and tradition of the Church.

Judge

In the last few years, I have begun my teaching year with the following statement, to pique student's interest (and hopefully begin the year with the challenge of the relevance of religion for them), and because I wholeheartedly believe it to be true. There is, in my mind, absolutely no coincidence that while religious affiliation declines, so has general happiness and mental wellbeing. The numbers of those suffering from depression and anxiety, the number of marriage breakdowns and suicides, can all be contributed to the decline of religious affiliation, or, at least, that which has taken its place – namely materialism. What benefit does big business get out of a faith that teaches its people to share good and service, that we will be judged on how much we loved God and one another, not on how much stuff we have? By removing religion from our lives, people feel the need to buy more rather than be more, and to do whatever it takes to get that stuff. St Augustine prays that 'our heart is restless until it rests in you'. We all have a restlessness, a whole in our heart, that must be filled. Without God to rest in, what else is there? Stuff, drama and gossip, conspiracy theories, honour, status, money, power. The list goes on.

I suppose on the flip side of that, where students know no better and have been raised in this secular materialistic world, religion just makes no sense. If everyone (sometimes and frustratingly teachers in a Catholic School can perpetuate this), is telling you that brands are important, that cars are important, that keeping up to date with TV shows that are designed to rot our brains, then why would students listen to a tradition that tells them the opposite? In a world where people continually seem to benefit from taking advantage of one another (clergy included), why would you love your neighbour? Not having a faith is the easy option, it is the option that means you can do what you want, be what you want, and act how you want without any 'oppression'. It is a battle where we are in the minority, and there are many factors that are hindering our ability to win.

As aforementioned, Bishop Barron claims the decline of young people in Church is the second biggest issue facing the Church. I could not agree more. In the Judge section of the SJA Process, we are asked to reflect on the issue by means of social analysis, which I have done in the previous two paragraphs (albeit brief). We are also to look at it theologically; what does the Church say about this issue. St Paul is an obvious source of inspiration because of his role in establishing and expanding the Church in its early years. In the First Letter to the Galatians, St Paul writes:

> *I am astonished that you are so quickly deserting the one who called you in the grace of Christ and are turning to a different gospel - not that there is another gospel, but there are some who are confusing you and want to pervert the gospel of Christ. But even if we or an angel from heaven should proclaim to you a gospel contrary to what we proclaimed to you, let that one be accursed! As we have said before, so now I repeat, if anyone proclaims to you a gospel contrary to what you received, let that one be accursed! Am I now seeking human approval, or God's approval? Or am I trying to please people? If I were still pleasing people, I would not be a servant of Christ.* [Gal 1 1:7-9 NRSVCE]

While commentary around this passage revolves more around Paul having to defend his credentials to the people of Galatia, it rings true to the issue we face today. This is but one of several examples of Paul's writing to the newly established communities, who were already being distracted by the alluring power of the devil.

In 2019, Pope Francis addressed this issue in his Christmas address, citing the rigidity of the Church as one of the reasons for the decline of religious affiliation. The inability of some to change their ways and respond to the signs of the times, one of the curses of clericalism, as he has said elsewhere, has led to 'Hatred and misunderstanding in a world where Christianity is increasingly irrelevant' (Winfield, 2019). 'Today we are no longer the only ones that produce culture, no longer the first nor the most listened to. The faith in Europe and in much of the West is no longer an obvious presumption but is often denied, derided, marginalized and ridiculed.' This is a scathing analysis and one which must be considered. How much can parents and educators do, when the Church is not coming to the party?

Act

Here, we come to the crux of my paper. We have looked at what is happening, discussed why it is happening and what the Church says about this issue, now we must act. How do we bring students back into the Church? How do we teach them that all that they know is contradictory to the way we are asked to live? How do we get them to fall in love with our Lord and His Church? In my experience, social action, using the critical thinking framework of SJA is the answer. Most students, and increasingly so, understand a plethora of social justice issues and want to do something about it. The 'Black Lives Matter' movement, and the 'School Strike 4 Climate Action', are but two that stand out amongst many in recent times. While there are some that are apathetic to any, if not all causes, there are more that are listening, reading, and researching these issues.

A framework is needed to guide these students to learn about these issues, reflect on it and then act. Or else, we end up with a surface level understanding, mediocre actions, and despondent children who have lost their passion. It is the Church's job to cultivate this love of neighbour and this care for creation. It is also an opportunity to teach the students this fact, and to introduce them to scripture, to the teachings of the Church, and to Catholic Social Teaching through their own interests and passions. This is what the SJA process provides. Not only do students learn about an issue in greater depth than anything that social media influencers, or bite-sized videos can provide (not to mention the quality/credibility of these sources of information), they also learn that the faith has so much to offer in ALL aspects of social justice and injustice. The Church was present and is present in all these fights for justice. Within our tradition, we have fought every fight, we have an answer for everything, we have a way of responding that is radical in its love and simple in its message.

Students learn about all of this while learning about the issue they care about. They begin to see that the Church is relational, the Church loves them and wants the best for them, and for all people. The dumbed down version of the faith they have received in the past is pushed aside and replaced with the idea of the Church being a beacon of Beauty, Truth and Goodness. They begin to see that the process, and therefore the tradition, can be applied not only in issues of justice, but when dealing with relational issues, wellbeing issues, business decisions, and so on. They begin to see what the Church has to offer for them in their lives, and then begin to see that they can learn about this every week (if not every day), in the Mass, where the priest offers a reflection every single day that is relevant to their lives. It is an 'in' for students that I have seen work time and time again.

A Case Study

When my wife and I made the decision to leave Melbourne for Hobart in 2017, one of my many tasks was to hand over the social justice program I had run at my school for 9 years. With the assistance of a supportive school and a visionary leader, I was able to create a social justice group that by the end of my time there, boasted 200 current students, and a network of 150 ex-students. There are many reasons for the success of the program; the time that I was allocated, the mentoring I received, the culture of the school. Without a doubt, however, one of the primary reasons was the format of *See, Judge, Act*.

Each year level would focus on a certain issue and work through the process. Sometimes we would have a SJA day, where we would work through the process and end the day with a list of possible actions. Sometimes, it would occur over several lunchtimes. Either way, students were aware of the importance of the process, and the power of it. Not only would it make the actions more impactful, varied, and organised, but it would make it hard for leadership to deny the requests to act as a thorough process had been undertaken to get the students to that point.

More than anything, however, was the power of the Judge section. We were able to teach students about the reasons issues existed; the root causes and the politics for example. We were also able to show students that the Church had something to say on the issue – the there are people out there who are driven by their love for God and one another to make a difference to the lives of so many, that the Bible was a source of moral wisdom and guidance that they could turn to anytime for anything. This was the affective outcome of the whole program, and I feel it was successful.

A great example of this is sharing a part of the Passion narrative in the Gospel according to John:

'When Jesus saw his mother and the disciple whom he loved standing beside her, he said to his mother, 'Woman, here is your son.' Then he said to the disciple, 'Here is your mother.' And from that hour the disciple took her into his own home.

I used this story with my social justice students and challenged them to think of themselves as that unknown disciple, and if Mary is now your mother, it means you are a sibling of Christ! Everyone, therefore, is a sibling of Christ! This is a powerful way to give them an understanding of why their passion to change the world is so important.

A highlight of my time at St Monica's College, Epping, was our Slow Fashion Exhibition, organised by our Year 9 Be More students in 2016. After learning about Fairtrade and ethical consumerism, each of the forty students researched a different ethical and sustainable clothing brand in Australia and asked them to let us borrow an item of clothing to be shown in an exhibition. Students organised a launch for the exhibition and then over 300 Year 9 students came through the exhibition over the space of a week to learn about the cost of the fast fashion industry on people and on the environment and then see what alternatives were out there. The students linked this to many of the messages from Laudato Si and the Catholic Social Teaching principle of stewardship, or integral ecology. Finally, students were given ideas on how to be more ethical in their daily lives, starting with looking after the things you have now.

Conclusion

I want nothing more than to lead the students in my care to a better understanding and a closer relationship with our Lord and His Church. I truly believe that the SJA process can do this in a powerful and relational way.

BOOKS AND ARTICLES CITED

- ABS. (2017). Religion in Australia: 2016 Census Data Summary. Canberra: ABS.
- Australian Bureau of Statistics. (2018). Census reveals Australia's religious diversity on World Religion Day. Canberra: Australian Bureau of

- Statistics. Retrieved from https://www.abs.gov.au/AUSSTATS/abs@.nsf/mediareleasesbyReleaseDate/8497F7A8E7DB5BEFCA25821800203DA4?OpenDocument
- Barron, B. (2019). Bishops, "Nones," and the Church: an Interview with Bishop Barron". Word on Fire. Baltimore: Word on Fire.
- Brigham, E. M. (2019). See, Judge, Act: Catholic Social Teaching and Service Learning [Revised Edition]. Minnesota: Anselm Academic.
- Clemmer, D. (2019, November 4). Evangelizing young 'nones' is Bishop Robert Barron's brand. National Catholic Reporter.
- Daintree, D. (2021). COLLOQUIUM 2021: Call for Papers. Retrieved from The Christopher Dawson Centre for Cultural Studies: https://www.dawsoncentre.org/colloquium-2015/
- Dantis, T., Bowell, P., Reid, S., & Dudfield, L. (2019). Listen to what the SPirit is Saying: Final Report for the Plenary Council Phase I: Listening and Dialogue. Canberra: Australian Catholic Bishops Conference & National Centre for Pastoral Research.
- Jensen, P. (2020, November 11). When it comes to religion, the Australian Census is asking the wrong questions. ABC Religion & Ethics.
- Mackay, H. (2016). Beyond Belief: How we find meaning, with or without religion. Sydney: Macmillan Australia.
- Pope Francis. (2020). Let Us Dream: The Path to a Better Future. London: Simon & Schuster.
- Pope Francis. (2020). Let Us Dream: The Path to a Better Future. London: Simon & Schuster.
- Pope John XXIII. (1961). Mater et Magistra: Encyclical of Pope John XXIII on Christianity and Social Progress. Vatican City: Vatican.

- Tao, Y., & Stapleton, T. (2018, July 11). Why the census fails to capture the religious identities of Asian Australians. Asian Currents.
- Willke, J. (1984). The Worker-Priest Experiment in France. America.
- Winfield, N. (2019, December 22). Pope denounces 'rigidity' as he warns of Christian decline. Associated Press.

CATHOLIC EDUCATION AND THE ASCENDANCE OF CHRISTIAN CULTURE

Gerard Gaskin

A Covenant Conception of Catholic Education

Formal Catholic education, as we see it today, builds upon an experiential legacy that spans centuries of human activity – the Church's work of living up to that divine command. But, Catholic education in its primordial form, also extends all the way back to the eternity of the divine Logos. Indeed, the Catholic understanding of education is far older than the two thousand years that have passed since Christ walked the earth. The central principle of Catholic education has its roots in the dawn of human existence and finds its first expression in the sacred Covenant between God and man.

Any discussion about Catholic Education cannot ignore the last will and testament (if we may call it that) of Jesus Christ. At the end of His earthly life, in full submission to the will of the Father Jesus commanded:

> *All authority in Heaven and earth has been given to me. Go, therefore, make disciples of all nations; baptise them in the name of the Father and of the Son and of the Holy Spirit, and teach them to observe all the commands I gave you. And look, I am with you always; yes, to the end of time.* (Matthew 28: 19-20)

The Church has a core mandate from God to proclaim salvation by bringing everyone to Christ. Catholic education is the jewel in the crown of the Catholic Church.

The Second Vatican Council affirms that education is primarily a spiritual activity, that true education contributes to the whole of the person: mind, body, soul, affectivity and emotions. The Council fathers were explicit about the fundamental nature of Catholic education. They describe it is an entirely spiritual activity with a supernatural purpose. You may be surprised to hear this – that the goals of education, even of education in the so-called secular subjects - mathematics, literacy and social, cultural and physical development, are entirely supernatural:

A Christian education does not merely strive for the maturing of a human person as just now described, but has as its principal purpose this goal: that the baptized, while they are gradually introduced the knowledge of the mystery of salvation, become ever more aware of the gift of Faith they have received, and that they learn in addition how to worship God the Father in spirit and truth.[1]

In short Catholic education aims:
- to bring Christ to our students and staff,
- to bring our students and staff to Christ, and through them,
- to bring Christ to the world.

In simple terms, this education is a personal encounter with the truth which of itself is sufficiently compelling to demand adherence. Hence, education is *existential* in the true sense – its operative realm is the personal experience of each participant. Precisely because it is the penetration of God (who is truth) into human existence, the message of the Gospel of Jesus Christ therefore has an intensely *formative*

---

[1] Second Vatican Council, *Gravissimum Educationis*. n. 2

trajectory, for teacher and learner alike. Learning cannot ever be anything but *experiential* and *personal*. Understood as a measurable cognitive gain within the subject, learning is a conscious process that engages sense, imagination, intellect, will and affective response. Religious education goes even further than this because it also has an explicit *moral purpose*, to form a conscience that will direct the person towards virtue – and towards salvation. Yet, this moral purpose has twofold expressions, - both of them intensely personal and both essential to the personal growth and formation of the human person – they are, firstly to form an abiding and intimate relationship with the person of Jesus Christ, and secondly, to so form one's conscience, within this intimacy and nourished by it, and in complete freedom, that one's only desire will be to do the will of Jesus. Within this idea resides everything that religious education needs, in order to be effective.

Writing in 1949, Christopher Dawson observed that Western civilization owed practically everything (its social institutions: education, law, government, the arts and culture) to Christianity and to a system of education that is an invitation of the young into the social and spiritual inheritance of the community. Dawson said:

> *However secularized our modern civilization may become, this sacred tradition remains like a river in the desert, and a genuine religious education can still use it to irrigate the thirsty lands and to change the face of the world with the promise of new life.*[2]

With great foresight, he warned that modern education stood in grave peril of eroding the very foundations upon

---

[2] Dawson, Christopher, *Understanding Europe*, (reprint) Washington: Catholic University of America Press, 2009, http://cuapress.cua.edu/res/images/books/frontmatter/DAUE.pdf (Accessed: 15/05/2014)

which our society had been built. That the attendant corrosion of religious belief we currently witness has become a reality, is now no longer a matter for speculation – but rather is now one of restoration and the need for urgent repair. He adds:

> *I do not think there is any need for me to insist on the fundamental thesis that the present crisis of Western civilization is due to the separation of our culture from its religious basis. I have been saying little else for the last fifteen years.*[3]

Dawson provides a useful caution that the enterprise of education ought to be ultimately, and uniquely, spiritual:

> *Christian education was not only an initiation into the Christian community, it was also an initiation into another world: the unveiling of spiritual realities of which the natural man was unaware and which changed the meaning of existence. And I think it is here that our modern education - including our religious education - has proved defective. There is in it no sense of revelation. It is accepted as instruction sometimes as useful knowledge, often as tiresome task work in preparation for some examination, but nowhere do we find that joyful sense of the discovery of a new and wonderful reality which inspired true Christian culture. All true religious education leads up to the contemplation of Divine Mysteries, and where this is lacking the whole culture becomes weakened and divided. It may be objected that this is the sphere of worship and not of education; but it is impossible to separate the two, since it was largely in the sphere of worship that the Christian tradition of education and culture arose and developed.*[4]

---

[3] Dawson, Christopher, *Education and the Crisis of Christian Culture*, Henry Regnery Company Illinois: 1949

[4] Dawson, Christopher. *The Crisis of Western Education* (The Works of Christopher Dawson). Washington: Catholic University of America Press, 2010, p. 10

A Faux Moral Imperative: Structural Societal Reform

Michael Fullan is a widely-recognised author on educational leadership for change. His published works span several decades and are considered to be essential reading for educational leaders and those seeking social change through education. Fullan sees himself as an educational reformer – part pedagogical practitioner and part social reformer – arguing that the former will bring about the latter. He sees education as caught up in a rapidly evolving social environment. *'The more complex society gets,'* he says, *'the more sophisticated leadership must become. Complexity means change, but specifically it means rapidly occurring, unpredictable, nonlinear change.'*[5]

Writing in 2001, introducing the term, *'leader's dilemma'* Fullan posits that failing to act when the environment around you is constantly changing leads to *'extinction';* whereas, making hasty decisions in conditions of *'mind racing mania'* can be equally fatal. While this introduction to his book 'Leading in a Culture of Change' is compelling and engaging, the philosophical and sociological assumptions it contains deserve careful attention.[6]

Further, his polemical style derives from the assertion that not to change in a changing environment is to face extinction. Whilst such a notion, derived as it is from evolutionary theory, may have wide credence in certain circles, it does require a little nuanced understanding when applied to the field of education.

---

[5] Fullan, M. *Leading in a Culture of Change.*, San Francisco, John Wiley and Sons. 2001 p. v.

[6] Quoting Robert Steinberg, Fullan says 'The essence of intelligence would seem to be in knowing when to thinks and act quickly, and knowing when to think and act slowly.' (Fullan, M. *Leading in a Culture of Change* p. vi.)

Michael Fullan's politico-utilitarian view of educational leadership is expressed with great power in the preface of his work *What's Worth Fighting for in the Principalship?* He explains that his work is about *'taking relentless action in the face of an amalgam of intersecting barriers and creating powerful levers for catapulting the system forward.'*[7] And so he quickly arrives at the fundamental crisis, *'The real reform agenda is societal development.'*[8]

Alma Harris, an English educational theorist, has also gained international recognition with her work on 'Distributed Leadership'. She predicates her case for system change on Fullan's *moral imperative*. 'This book', says Harris, *'is primarily concerned with addressing the educational apartheid that separates the rich from the poor so starkly in terms of educational attainment.'*[9]

A footnote to this discussion is briefly to consider whether educational reform for social equality is really a moral imperative at all. Historically, Marxist ideology has understood the class struggle as a moral imperative. Without suggesting that Fullan and Harris are Marxist ideologues, nevertheless it is clear that they do seek a specifically re-structured social order. They desire to so re-configure the nation's educational system so that it will result in a society where the income gap between rich and poor is minimized. They are also quite prepared to exploit the touch points of real educational power, the educational leaders, to achieve this aim. Harris is quite explicit about her agenda for structural social reform:

---

[7] Fullan, M., *What's Worth Fighting for in the Principalship?* (Second Edition) New York, Teachers College Press, Columbia University. 2008 p. vii.

[8] Fullan, M. *Turnaround Leadership.*, Jossey-Bass, San Francisco. 2006p. p. 1

[9] Harris, A., Distributed School Leadership: Developing Tomorrow's Leaders., London, Routledge. 2009 p. 3.

Closing the attainment gap will not be secured simply by providing more school leaders. This will only be achieved by ameliorating the negative and pervasive social and economic conditions that influence communities and the life chances of young people. Many attempts at educational improvement can only be part, and possibly only a small part, of the wider agenda of reducing social and economic inequalities in society.[10]

Sounds a bit like class warfare to me.

Fullan too, is equally explicit about his desire to create a new society – even using the Marxist term, the collective:

But for education reform, it should be clear that the moral imperative focuses on raising the bar and closing the gap in student learning and achievement for all children regardless of background. It is about a better society for individuals and for the collective.[11]

Christopher Dawson, writing more than half a century before Fullan and Harris, would say of such an ideological stance:

What a mess these clever devils have made of our world. No doubt the real source of the evil is to be found not in the universalisation of education, but in the destruction of the old hierarchy of Divinity, Humanity and Natural Science that was the tradition of European higher education. The real evil of popular education was not so much its secularism, but its Utilitarian character.[12]

Dawson's observations could not be more salient in an educational world that now values inclusion (narrowly defined as unquestioning acceptance of every radical agenda), diversity (similarly defined as the imperative to

---

[10] Harris, A., *Distributed School Leadership*. Op. Cit. p. 4.
[11] Fullan, M., *The Moral Imperative Realized*. p. x-ix.
[12] Dawson, Christopher, *Education and the Crisis of Christian Culture*, Henry Regnery Company Illinois: 1949

embrace rampant and deviant, sterile, sexual self-gratification, no matter how repulsive) LGBTI+ radical sexuality, gender theory and a pronoun-obsessed tyranny of language, the like of which has not been seen since 1940's Germany.

Writing in 1949, Christopher Dawson made the chilling prophecy that this post-war intensification of educational effort would be compelled by strong, competitive, crypto-Marxist socio-political motives:

> *It is possible that after the war we shall see a great intensification of educational effort, especially in the East and in the non-European world. But behind this there will be a strong competitive socio-political motive similar to that which inspired the educational efforts of the Soviets during the past twenty years. At its best this means the raising of the standard of life for all the backward and exploited peoples and classes; at its worst it may mean no more than mass conditioning of populations for purposes of power politics. But in either case there is the same danger of an over-emphasis on the utilitarian motive and a neglect of the deeper spiritual forces which have been the creative element in all the great cultures of the past, whether Christian or non-Christian.*[13]

Pope Benedict sounded a similar caution about believing that man's future good resides in rebuilding the social structures in this way. In his encyclical on the theological virtue of hope he stated:

> *The right state of human affairs, the moral well-being of the world can never be guaranteed simply through structures alone, however good they are. Such structures are not only important, but necessary; yet they cannot and must not marginalize human freedom. Even the best*

---

[13] Dawson, C., *Education and the Crisis of Christian Culture.* Op. Cit. p. 7.

structures function only when the community is animated by convictions capable of motivating people to assent freely to the social order.[14]

A crusade for social structural change is at odds with a personal Christian faith because the right state of human affairs, the moral well-being of the world, can never be guaranteed simply through structures alone, however well-intentioned they may be. This search for power-in-leadership will create an inevitable dissonance, when those elements, designed as they are for a precise and explicit social change wherever they are appropriated into a Catholic concept of education.

A Solution: Do Education Better

At its best, Catholic Education is an immersion into a rich and universal history and culture for our students. They can only benefit from being absorbed in the immense wealth and breadth of the accumulated cultural patrimony of Catholic life and history. Not only does such an approach engage the senses in a tangible way, in expressing the underlying truths of our Faith but it also deepens their cultural understanding of the influence of the faith they share with the people of history.

As Christian educators, if we are to counter the secularising and de-personalising influences around us, we must re consider re-weaving the long, golden threads of human experience, culture and learning into the everyday curriculum. Some of these content threads are:

---

[14] Pope Benedict XVI, *Spe Salvi, Encyclical Letter*, 2007.
http://www.vatican.va/holy_father/benedict_xvi/encyclicals/doc uments/hf_ben-xvi_enc_20071130_spe-salvi_en.html (Accessed: 02/01/2013), n. 24 (a & b)

Christian Vocabulary - induction into the unique lexicon of Catholic terms and ideas – related to the relevant content being taught in Core teachings;

Sacred Scripture - a comprehensive understanding of Old and New Testaments, Salvation history and the manner in which the old testament pre-figures the new, and the new testament completes the old in the person of Jesus.

Christian Art - an aesthetic appreciation of the specific pedagogy and history of Christian art and iconography as expressed in stained glass, painting and statuary;

Christian Architecture - to appreciate the evolving aesthetics and engineering innovations that underlie some of the world's greatest cathedrals;

Christian Literature - the rich patrimony of poetry, morality plays and dramatic recreations of momentous events in Church history which are a means of expressing Christian truths;

Christian Music - to build an understanding and appreciation of the beauty of Christian music - choral, plainsong, liturgical, operatic and orchestral;

Christian History – the ability to see oneself as being *part of* the epic and sweeping timeline of the people and major events of Church History that shaped world events and provided the social institutions which endure to this day – from the first covenant of God with man, to the missionary journeys of the Apostles to the present media phenomenon of the papacy

Christian Prayer - immersion into the Church's rich history of prayer - from the psalms to monastic chant and the traditional prayers and devotions of history and today;

Christian Heroes - the Saints and Martyrs who inspire and teach us about how to live and die as faithful Christians, including the martyrs of the French Revolution and the Spanish Civil War;

Christian Mysticism - an exploration of the wealth of Christian religious experience, of prayer, both contemplative and apostolic, from the asceticism of the desert fathers to contemporary religious life; and an understanding of how monasticism helped to shape civilisation, culture, agriculture, science law and education.

The greatest of all these is the last: sacramental experience and the *mystagogical encounter*. The liturgy, designed for the worship of God and the divinisation of humanity, is in part, a sensory, and consequently *affective*, experience. As the Second Vatican Council teaches:

In the liturgy the sanctification of the man is signified by signs perceptible to the senses, and is effected in a way which corresponds with each of these signs; in the liturgy the whole public worship is performed by the Mystical Body of Jesus Christ, that is, by the Head and His members.[15]

It is no accident that the incarnational/corporeal elements of the liturgy appeal to our human sensitivities: the silences during times of prayer and recollection; the symbolic gestures of the priest's hands and bodily posture, signifying supplication, petition and thanksgiving; the sacred music and song, written to magnify prayer; the elements of water, bread, wine and oil denoting, at different times, our self-giving and God's sublime gifts. Indeed, the sacred art and architecture designed to adorn the liturgical mysteries, along with fragrant incense, provide a complete sensory expression of the sacramental realities which they signify. However, these elements exist, not to provide corporeal satisfaction to the participants; but rather, to express outwardly the inner actions of God's grace at work in the sanctification of humanity; as such, they *educate*.

As the principal means of grace, the Eucharistic liturgy provides affective, intellectual and spiritual nourishment. Christian formation and education would be impoverished without it. Because we are made in the image and likeness of God our participation in the liturgy conforms us closely with

---

[15] Sacrosanctum Concilium, n. 7 §3

Jesus Christ. Regular liturgical/sacramental life makes us more like Christ. The Fathers of the Second Vatican Council said:

> *From this it follows that every liturgical celebration, because it is an action of Christ the priest and of His Body which is the Church, is a sacred action surpassing all others; no other action of the Church can equal its efficacy by the same title and to the same degree.*[16]

The *mystagogical catechesis* of the liturgy is an aspect of Christian formation which involves practically no formal, *classroom learning*, yet it is powerfully (supernaturally) formative. It enlightens the mind and speaks to the heart invisibly by incorporating us ever more intimately with our Saviour. The grace of Christ gives light to our understanding and moves our affectivity to be increasingly receptive to the Word of God and to live it. For this reason alone, sacramental life is an indispensable dimension of religious education.

Catholic Doctrine: Indispensable to Culture

In the typical school subjects of Maths, Science, Literacy etc the natural termini are: knowledge, understanding, attitudes beliefs, skills and application – from surface, to deep to the point of transfer. We expect students to emerge from a Maths education with mathematical process-knowledge and skills, and a sense of the value of mathematics in daily life. I suppose most of us would be pleased to see a student emerging from the study of English to have the competence to read and comprehend David Copperfield, to appreciate the social, historical and literary context of Dickens' novels and writing, to discuss the moral implications of Dickens' social critique and to be able to

---

[16] Sacrosanctum Concilium, n. 7 §4

express these things using cogent English, spelling and punctuation – perhaps, even to argue the relative merits of the book versus the movie.

These are the natural secular subjects, the ones we need if we are to function effectively in human society, and able to make some positive contribution to its growth and development. Notwithstanding their immense value in the liberal arts curriculum, their termini - their ends - remain always precisely within the natural realm. There is only one school subject that deals *entirely* in the supernatural. That subject is Catholic religious education.

The natural terminus of Catholic education is life eternal - because, after death, that's the only thing there is - eternity. Religious education is the only school subject that dares to teach the doctrines about the hidden life of the soul and to claim knowledge of the after-life - believing these eternal verities to be real and true – not just empty literary images. Religious education is the only subject that grounds social justice in its first principles, explaining its true impetus as proceeding from the innate dignity and inalienable rights of the human person, given by God. Religious education - in its dissemination, appreciation and appropriation of Catholic doctrine - is the only subject with the capacity to connect each student with their immeasurable Christian cultural and intellectual heritage – the true, the good and the beautiful – all the while steeped in belief and love for God.

Religious education is the only subject where the defence of innocent unborn life can be grounded in God's law, itself the foundation of the fundamental human right to life. Religious education is the only subject that can provide students with the comprehensive doctrinal and ethical/moral framework needed to be able to judge right from wrong in a society that, at times, presents vice as virtue and denigrates religious belief as no more than superstition, or as a *fundamentalism* that confounds the libertarian exercise of absolute freedom. Religious education is the only subject that can explain the deepest sacramental connections between liturgical worship of the Creator, the Sanctifier and the Redeemer with lived human experience. Religious education is the only subject that can ignite the fire of love of God in our students so that they can live heroic lives for the benefit of others.

We might say that RE is the formation of our students for this life and for the next. A priest friend of mine used to say, 'We Christians straddle the divide between nature and supernature; our feet are firmly planted in this life, while our eyes are on the next.' Whilst we live and move and have our being in this natural world, our hearts and minds are fixed on the next one. After all, that's what gives all the reason to the good that we do here on earth.

Supernatural Education

Yet supernature is with us right now. The fact that we cannot see it, even though it exists, in something as familiar as the day-to-day liturgy, does not mean that it is inaccessible, but rather that it is waiting to be accessed - waiting for its beauty and transcendence to be unlocked, explained, experienced – to transform lives.

Imagine if every Catholic teacher really viewed their day-to-day professional activity, not in terms of knowledge acquisition, not in terms of success criteria ticked off, or of curriculum compliance satisfied, but rather in terms of how many of her students order their daily lives towards attaining eternal life? Sounds crazy in this hyper-wired, switched-on, blue-toothed secular age? In a world of rapidly changing forces, such that we cannot even imagine the cultural, scientific and political milieu into which this year's class of Kinder kids will graduate (14 years from now) can we be sure of anything?

If those in the vanguard of ideologies committed to re-defining the intrinsic status of human relationships and the family, can recruit enough of us to their cause to fulfil their wildest dreams, will mathematics, science or history be able to save a society that may, by then, have resolutely turned its back on the most basic human institutions?

Can literacy, or for that matter science, enable us to realise that awesome salvific promise made by a Middle Eastern preacher who died on a cross and rose from the dead twenty centuries ago? In a society where our taxes pay for the slaughter of 90,000 Australian boys and girls a year – that's 250 innocent lives per day per day – can art or music defend them? Who will remind a cynical, crumbling post-modern culture of our destiny to unfathomable greatness? Who will sing of that Covenant promise that echoes, from the dawn of the chosen people, even now through the centuries, 'I will be with you, even to the close of the age'? Who will witness to a life of virtue and charity in a society that no longer cherishes such things? Who will strive for beatitude for no better reason than because of a 'beatitudes' speech made by one person so long ago on a desolate and almost forgotten mountainside?

I contend that of all our school subjects, it is only religious education that is remotely capable of speaking to these realities. It is an awesome reality, in the true sense of the word awesome, to realise that the human and natural school subjects we teach in our schools today, although deeply worthy, are yet so finite and limited, ultimately incapable of building the interior spiritual lives of our students simply because these natural subjects cannot transcend their natural limits.

The Congregation for Catholic Education recently admonished Catholic educators to give the necessary kind of witness that can rise above the *dismal effects* of our secular society. Citing the *spiritual poverty* of contemporary culture, its authors challenged Catholic school leaders, in powerful terms, that they must be *inspired* by the Gospel, outstanding in pedagogy and capable of resisting the seductive *fashionability* of today's culture.[17]

How can we live up to these expectations? Every Catholic education system is already gifted with the only thing that it needs to cherish and nurture, a precious gift with unfettered potential to change lives and which has, over the ages, truly changed the world, something that exceeds the natural subjects. We are called to form our students in a special kind of knowledge – not just any knowledge – but the only knowledge that contains the truths that set us free – supernatural knowledge - nothing less than the revealed self-knowledge of our all-loving God.

God's self-revelation to us is perfect self-expression given to us for only one reason: that we may be led to repent and believe and live the Gospel. God's self-expression, gifted via Sacred Scripture and Scared Tradition, which we know as *doctrine* (a word that carries within it the root of all teaching and learning: *docere* = to teach) is not made from empty formulas but living ideas - breathing no other life than that of their sublime author, the maker of everything that exists - He who breathed everything into existence. Knowledge banishes ignorance. The more we know someone, the more

---

[17] *Spiritual poverty and declining cultural levels are starting to produce their dismal effects, even within Catholic schools. Often times, authoritativeness is being undermined. It is really not a matter of discipline – parents greatly appreciate Catholic schools because of their discipline – but do some Catholic school heads still have anything to say to students and their families? Is their authority based on formal rules or on the authoritativeness of their testimony? If we want to avert a gradual impoverishment, Catholic schools must be run by individuals and teams who are inspired by the Gospel, who have been formed in Christian pedagogy, in tune with Catholic schools' educational project, and not by people who are prone to being seduced by fashionability, or by what can become an easier sell, to put it bluntly.* Congregation for Catholic Education *Educating Today and Tomorrow: A Renewing Passion*, Part (III) 1. (a) §3

we can love the person. Knowledge of God: his promise of undying love and his invitation to intimacy – these are the doctrines we give to children – because they are the truths will that will set them free (John 8:32)

This precious type of knowledge is not static or stagnant. It contains within itself a powerful dynamism, one which only finds its completion in acts of intellect and will: in personal belief and conscious act. Knowledge of doctrine for its own sake is pointless. Knowledge of the doctrine that resonates with God's personal call to each of us is priceless because it refuses to let us remain static. Here, alone, lies the future of Catholic education. Graced with the divine life of God Himself, it is a complete education, one which compels us towards the expansion and ever fuller expression of our Baptismal faith – to lives of sacrament, service and salvation.

SHIFTING THE PARADIGM OF INITIAL TEACHER TRAINING:
The Hub Cohort Model for Teacher Training in Australian Christian Affiliated Schools

David Hastie

Part One: The Challenges
'Teacher education is the Dodge City of the education world'[1]

Australian Church / school international exceptionalism

Church and school have always been, and continue to be, intimately entwined in post 1788 Australia. Australia has the fifth highest non- government per capita proportion of schools in the world, and the highest access to school choice in the world (Musset 2012). Over 90% of Australian non-government schools are Christian-affiliated. This constitutes ~1.3 million students in 2018, out of a total school age population of ~3.9 million. Around 40% of all secondary school enrolments are in non-government schools. (ABS, 2019)[2]

---

[1] Levine, A. *Educating School Teachers*, New York, 2006: The Education Schools Project.

[2] The highest is in Victoria, at 43%. Over the last decade, there has been an average increase of enrolments in Victorian independent schools at the primary into secondary transition point, of 62% (ABS, 2019): figures

Australian Governments are clearly committed to sustaining these schools, sometimes for ideological, but mostly logistical reasons: there is planned economic state under-provision in education, nationwide. Non-government school fees contribute an annual saving of well over $11 billion to State and Commonwealth budgets (AIS 2018).

This represents significant market opportunity for Australian Christian affiliated schooling, but also a weighty responsibility towards the flourishing of both church and state. This realisation of such opportunity is by no means certain, however, not least because of challenges related to strategic HR.

This paper will not only argue that 8 HR challenges face high quality teacher supply into Australian faith-affiliated schools, but that several of these challenges create instability across Australian teacher work-force planning in general, and to understand the former, one must see it as a subset of the latter.

The paper then indicates the solution of *Formation in subsidiarity* or *'Training on country, for country'*, and briefly signals that the existing St Phillip's Christian School *Teaching School* model in the NSW Hunter, The Teaching School Alliance Sydney, and the St Thomas Aquinas Teaching School in Tasmania constitutes the best future direction for guaranteeing strategic HR stability in Australian Schools in general, and Christian faith-affiliated schools in particular.

Challenge 1: Lack of supply of ethos-aligned Christian teachers[3]

Despite Australia's uniquely high non-government enrol-

---

are derived and analysed from the ABS table 42b.

[3] The topic has not been formally researched or published in peer-reviewed format. The unpublished data for this section has been collected through my own meetings from July 2017- August 2019 with:

ment proportions, Christian affiliated schools find themselves significantly under-prepared to rise to the government's needs, in two key areas: HR, and efficient new school planting. School planting is a topic for another paper, but the key HR problem in Christian- affiliated schools is a straightforward supply and demand issue: the uniquely large size of the sector creates a high demand for ethos-aligned staff that current Australian teacher supply cannot effectively meet. There are simply not enough high-quality confessional Christian teachers on the open Australian job market, to supply the sector.

It must be recognised that there is not one definition of what constitutes a Christian teacher, nor Christian school. However, this paper generally includes schools that publicly

---

the assistant directors of the Catholic education offices of Tasmania, Wilcannia –Forbes, Wagga Wagga and Armidale; the Executive director of Edcomm; the CEO / COO/ HR Director of The Anglican Schools Corporation (TASC); The CEO and Board of CEN Australia; the VIC/ TAS/ NSW/ QLD/ WA State SEOS and Executive Officer of CSA; The Executive Director of Associated Christian Schools; The CEO of CCM schools network; the chair of ISCA; the CEO and Associate Chief Executive of AIS NSW; The CEO of AISSA; Associate Dean, Academic, School of Education, of Notre Dame University Sydney; Associate Dean, Academic, School of Education, of Notre Dame University Freemantle; The President and Academic Dean of Campion College; The President and Dean of Education of Christian Heritage College; The President and Dean of Education of Tabor College Adelaide; the Dean of Education of Eastern College; The President and Dean of Education of Morling College; The CEO of SCEA WA; The Principal of VOSE College WA; The CEO and executive of Christian Schools Tasmania; The Right Reverend Greg Anderson, Anglican Bishop of the Northern Territory; the State SEO of CEN Tasmania; many other academics in Christian Tertiary; direct conversations with 127 school principals (NSW:65; VIC:18; QLD:25; SA: 8; WA: 8; NT:2); and many other board members and staff from over in all states and territories across all price point varieties of the Australian independent schooling movement.

align their missions to the claims, rites, requirements, lifestyles, communions, scriptures and loves of classical Christian orthodoxy. A 'Christian Teacher', would thus be defined as one whose personal faith confessional life and vocational motives, sufficiently align with classical Christian orthodoxy, at least to the extent that the mission of the school can be efficiently embedded without significant disruption and mistrust of staff. These definitions would include most Catholic schools, many Anglican Schools, many other denominational schools, and almost all non-denominational Christian Schools. (Hastie 2012)

In most areas outside of the narrowing bible belts of Sydney, Melbourne, and the Gold Coast, the lack of HR supply has generally been met in two ways.

Firstly, to revert when necessary to employing demonstrably non-Christian staff. Secondly, when faced with a choice between professionally mediocre Christian teacher, or an excellent non-Christian teacher, to preference the appointment of the ethos-aligned Christian.

It is widely recognised in the sector that both practices are a source of frustration for many school principals and school boards, but are widely endured through sheer necessity-there are not enough high quality ethos-aligned Christian teachers. Both practices can have significant impact on the mission of schools, in the following ways.

Older denominational schools have both explicit and tacit contracts with parents of high academic performance, and other cultural capital guarantees, and thus are typically more likely to appoint a non-Christian teacher on the basis of quality when faced with a lack of high-quality Christian option. Owing to a range of reasons, staff churn in high price-point independent schools is comparatively lower, and hence this appointment is likely to stay in a Christian affiliated grammar school for over a decade, potentially embedding secularity deep within the culture of certain sections of the school.

A poor quality teacher in a low fee Christian or Catholic Christian school (or any school, for that matter), on the other hand, can lead to enrolment loss, cultural disturbance, significant increases in transaction costs as trust breaks down, and a waste of leadership time. It also often leads to expensive industrial relations legal scenarios.

In short, the under-supply of ethos-aligned Christian teachers is a HR pressure point for Australian Christian affiliated schooling, and the religious mission of these schools is constantly exposed to this pressure. In this milieu schools are tending to operate in an operational, or *reactive* HR mode, rather than a strategic HR mode.

Challenge 2: Big Secularism

Amongst Australian secularists are many who have sought over the years to constrict the scope and influence of Australian faith-affiliated schools. This has been, historically, via various campaigns to restrict government funding (Maddox, 2013, 2014 a-g; Caro and Bonner 2007). These campaigns have been unsuccessful, probably owing to the budgetary benefits of non-government schools already noted. Indeed non-government sector enrolments have displaced government school enrolments by an annual average of 0.2% for a period of three decades[4] (ABS 2019).

However on 17 October, Australian Greens Senator Richard Di Natale introduced the 'Discrimination Free Schools Bill 2018' into the Federal Senate, which would 'remove the exemption for faith-based educational

---

[4] Until 2015, this was an unbroken trend for over 30 years there has been a reversion of .1% enrolments annually back to state schools since 2015, largely created by a slight reversal of the traditional trend of new migrant population growth absorption into Catholic primary schools in Vic. A slight decline also occurred in TAS, WA and SA, but seem to track alongside decline in State school enrolments (ABS, 2019). Independent School Enrolments have continued to increase unabated in all states and territories.

institutions to discriminate against students and teachers' (Legal and Constitutional Affairs References Committee, 2018:5). The bill was defeated, but in November 2018 the Labor and Australian Greens controlled Senate Standing Committees on Legal and Constitutional Affairs, conducted a surprise and rapid inquiry into 'Legislative exemptions that allow faith-based educational institutions to discriminate against students, teachers and staff' (Parliament of Australia 2018a). After an unconscionably brief 13 day submissions period (13 November-26th November), and only one public hearing,[5] the inquiry found that existing exemptions to the Commonwealth Sex Discrimination Acts should be rescinded. Despite an extensive dissenting report (50 pages), and many of the 180 submissions alarmed by the sudden and rapid pace of the inquiry, Labor Senator Penny Wong introduced legislation three days later that would have removed the right of Christian schools to be exempted from the Commonwealth Sex Discrimination Act when dealing with gay and transgender students and staff (Parliament of Australia 2018b). The bill was narrowly defeated in the Senate, but was followed by the Labor Party's election commitment that all exemptions would be removed if they won government in the 18 May 2019 general election, an eventuality that seemed highly likely - until election night.[6]

The furore around the October- November 2019 inquiries and bills, indicated to all that the capacity to restrict the already insufficient supply of ethos-aligned Christian staff

---

[5] Given the short consultation period, it would have been virtually impossible for the committee to have read all of the submissions before writing the report, which was extensive. It is a fair and reasonable hypothesis to hold that the report was a largely pre-prepared, forgone conclusion, and was in part designed to demonstrate that the Government could not control a majority, as a government member – Julia Banks- had recently defected to the cross benches.

[6] The proposed legislation was arguably one of the discreet causes of the surprise return of the conservative government in the May 2019 election (Hastie 2018).

through the instrument of industrial anti-discrimination law, represents a significant potential challenge to the explicit missions of many Christian- affiliated schools. This is not because of any particular agenda to deny education to transgender or gay students: there have been few legal cases in Australia where this has been claimed, and certainly none supported in the courts (Hastie, 2018b). The pressure on mission, rather, came with the restriction of faith-affiliated schools to appoint staff who aligned in belief and lifestyle to their particular credos.

Yet even if schools maintain the legal right to exclusively employ ethos aligned Christian staff, there is actually no guarantee that this will ensure the Christian mission of schools, owing to two factors: the secular paradigm of many Australian University teacher training degrees, and the lack of effective induction into Christian education distinctives in existing Christian affiliated schools.

The dominant paradigm of Australian ITE training, furthermore, is frequently founded on derivations of Critical theory and Marxist theory. Marxist and Critical theory may be classified as conflict theories, or 'emancipatory' theories (Symes and McIntyre, 2000), characterising society and history as consisting primarily of a power struggle between oppressor and oppressed. Such approaches are significant and valid in the history and theorising of Christian education, indeed all education. Perhaps the most foundational text of Neo Marxist education, Paulo Friere's *Pedagogy of the oppressed*, was written for teachers working amongst indigenous poor under the 1970s Brazilian fascist juntas, and is itself a form of Christian liberation theology[7].

---

[7] However, the intra-historical eschatology and collectivist doctrine of salvation of Freire and his theological contemporaries is regarded by many as an extreme departure from classical Christianity, including orthodox Catholicism, Anglicanism and a wide variety of Evangelical Protestantism. Indeed these early forms of liberation theology have been regularly censured by presiding bodies of global

The Neo Marxist paradigm has been additionally augmented in recent education theory by the social capital liberation theories of Bourdieu (Bourdieu, 1992, 1986), and the hyper-postmodernist libertarianism of Michel Foucault (Foucault, 1992, 1977). It is arguable, however, that in the Australian context, a fusion of emancipatory paradigms, juxtaposed with the extraordinarily high social prosperity and high distributed social wage, renders the emancipatory approach to education somewhat redundant as a dominant paradigm in ITE. However, when lacking the context of economic poverty, Critical and neo-Marxist approaches do not, as might be reasonably expected, recede, but continue by dint of their inner design to move onto a different 'host' cause (Hastie, 2010). Relative to Friere's original context, and most other nations past and present, there are far fewer poor Australian students; a country with the world's highest GDP, on a number of measures, and possibly the richest generation who have lived in the history of the world (Credit Suisse, 2018; Gal and Bruek, 2018).[8] Consequently, the focus of 'emancipatory' education theory enmeshed in many Australian Teacher training programmes in the Australian context, has tended to shift from targeting economic oppression, to proxy targeting any institutional authority that makes claims upon personal individualistic agency.

In this climate, ITE students have been taught in a range of ways and courses that that Christianity should be relegated to the private sphere, or often that religion itself is socially toxic, and best eliminated from schools. In many recent public debates, the Critical theory paradigm has become

---

denominations, including the Vatican's Congregation for the Doctrine of the Faith (CDF, 1985).

[8] This is not to say that there are significant issues of poverty amongst some small sections of the Australian population, nor to suggest that seeking to alleviate and rectify this situation is unnecessary. To the contrary, the *Hub* model as described later in this paper, is already addressing such issues in the NSW Hunter, and is being explored for implementation in remote indigenous communities.

more evident, with the depiction of Christianity as an oppressor, an ideology that harms children, and harms social diversity (Hastie, 2018; Ongly, 2015; Wood, 2015a,b; Australian Broadcasting Corporation, 2013; Browne, 2015; Carson, 2015; Cox, 2013; Greenwich, 2013a, b; McIlroy, 2013)

Placing a young adult of Christian faith thus secularly trained, in front of a classroom, and anticipating they will manage teaching a specialized curriculum from a Christian worldview is, at best, an ambitious expectation. This has been widely recognised in Australian Christian affiliated schooling, but insufficiently addressed.

Challenge 3: The insufficiency of retro-fitting Christian worldview for staff in schools

The most purposeful Christian schools operate Christian education retrofits and inductions, in an attempt to re-orientate staff after four years of secular instruction. However these programmes typically operate for about a week a year. There is no systematic research I am aware of into the effectiveness of Christian education retrofits in independent schools.

There are some concerted attempts: The National Institute of Christian Education MEd programmes (NICE, 2019), their curriculum development tool *Transformation by design* (CEN 2019); The CSA resource *Locating learners in God's big story* (CSA, 2019) the Sydney Anglican Education Commission (Edcomm, 2019) courses and conferences; the Focus on Faith Course in The Anglican Schools Corporation (TASC)[9]. These are all purposeful and thorough initiatives, but the structural models of these organisations do not

---

[9] This resource is not publically available, but is well known to the author, who had occasional oversight of administering the course, whilst employed as Education Strategist for The Anglican Schools Corporation (2015-2017).

mandate participation of schools, and are hence unable to ensure a common standard.

It is reasonable to say, however, that many Christian schools are unable or unwilling to direct resources towards purposeful 'retrofitting' training.[10] The widespread default behaviour, in practice, tends to an unverified industrial assumption: try as hard as one can to employ a quality, ethos aligned Christian teacher, put them into a classroom, and hope for the best.

Challenge 4: 'Ethos alignment' is a problem across all school sectors.

However, there are many other elements to 'ethos' in individual Christian faith-affiliated schools that are highly dependent on other elements of culture and demographics. I would argue that widespread complaints about a lack of 'classroom readiness', in ITE graduates (TEMAG, 2014: xviii), is largely code for 'lack of alignment' of the graduate to the realities of the particular school site, which in large part means 'ethos'- alignment.

Contrast, for example, the most useful faith-oriented approach that one might need, in dealing with indigenous 12 year olds at St Therese Catholic Community School in Wilcannia, in remote far western NSW (St Therese's, 2019),

---

[10] There is no systematic research I am aware of the effectiveness of teacher re-Christianisation programmes in independent schools. When specifically asked about this during my 2012 PhD research on English teachers in NSW Protestant schools- across a sample of 139 teachers, I found that the regular input at a faculty level- which is where specialised Christian education would occur - was largely non-existent. Indeed, non-denominational Christian schools faculties effectively only met an average maximum of three times a term. The denominational schools in my sample were better at having fortnightly faculty meetings, but no participants from this sub-sample reported training around Christian worldview at a faculty level.

to the requirement to supervise Saturday sport at, say, the high fee St Andrew's Cathedral School, located at the centre of the Sydney CBD (St Andrew's Cathedral School, 2019). Both can be seen to be intrinsically linked to the faith mission of those schools, but require a significantly different ethos in staff members, in fact probably an entirely different temperament and staff member altogether. One type of ethos-aligned Christian teacher does fit all sites.

After all, staff ethos alignment, and formation towards and into it, is actually a contemporary challenge for most Australian Schools, including state schools. All effective schools are driven by a coherent culture (Mohammed, 2009; Fullan, 2004), and all coherent culture is driven by an ethos, to which staff need to be effectively oriented, a staff of high proficiency and low turnover. One cannot establish an effective quality learning culture without these basic guarantees. It is erroneous to conceive of Christian mission as something disentangled from all of the other learning and cultural elements in a Christian- affiliated school.

If school culture/ ethos is held to be, not as a generic or homogenous phenomenon across Australian schools, but something that is profoundly site-specific and localised, then HR challenges facing Christian affiliated schools, can actually be understood as a subset of generalised workforce-planning challenges facing Australian teaching.

There are many well developed methods of describing and measuring 'coherent culture' in educational and organisational research. Alphacrucis College's *Centre for the Future of Schooling* is currently focusing on social capital theory (SCT) across several projects and clusters of research students. The AC preference for SCT is driven by its capacity to measure relational elements to bonded communities, a necessary alignment to the AC graduate attributes (Alphacrucis College, 2019) and the faith-orientation of the college. According to Onyx and Bullen:

Social capital may be generated anywhere when the conditions for its production are satisfied, that is, wherever there are dense, lateral networks involving voluntary engagement, trust, and mutual benefit. (2000: 39)

According to SCT, coherent school culture –indeed any group culture- flourishes best when mechanisms of profound 'bonding and bridging capital' exist: participation in networks, reciprocity, trust, social norms, the commons, and social agency. (Onyx and Bullen 2000; Etzioni 1996; Putnam, 1995; Fukiyama, 1995). The role of strategic HR, or 'strategic fit' in establishing, sustaining and increasing this 'bonding capital' is central, now widely recognised in broad industry improvement theories such as *High Performing Work Systems* (Yan Jiang and Lieu, 2014).

If the pursuit of high quality, coherent school cultures is a central concern in Australian education, not only Christian affiliated schooling needs to reconsider how better to align its training to the actual workforce needs, the entire Australian school education system needs to reconsider its workforce planning.

To sustainably achieve this form of 'bridging capital' in the formation of bonded networks, however, requires a major paradigm shift throughout the entire narrative of the Australian education social contract. This is long overdue. The dominant narrative of homogenous, massified and centrally administered schooling was actually designed in the 1880s, and amended slightly in the 1960's. In this account, the norm is constituted by a comprehensive 'free, compulsory and secular' state school, lying at the heart of a tightly geographically circumscribed, and localized community, across which boundaries citizens were not permitted to stray, both by law and by the tacit assent that schooling choice was the aberration from the norm. There was little school choice in this long-held discourse (circa 1880-1975), with a dominant liberal democratic Anglo-Protestant tribal sect at the core of the establishment of state schools (Piggin and Linder, 2018; Hastie 2017). This dominant vision of citizenship was self-policing, the Catholic minority generally marginalized through a century of deep sectarianism, having withdrawn into its own ideological enclosure of systemic Catholic schools in the 1880-1890s. Only the wealthy few would pursue the option of high fee elite private schools, long viewed with suspicion and increasing hostility by generations of advocates of the Social Democratic centralised state schooling model.

Circumstances have significantly changed, however, and new problems have arisen. The forced government imposition of homogenous, massified and centrally administered schooling ('free, compulsory and secular') was essential, when the public instruction acts were established in the 1880s, reducing mass-illiteracy and non-school attendance in the chaos of the colonial period, particularly following the 1851-1880 gold rushes. (Hastie, 2017). It was also needed to expand this public guarantee to high school aged children under the NSW Wyndham scheme (and its inter-state equivalents) in the 'post-war Keynesean settlement' (Campbell and Sherrington, 2006:98). Yet, even though it is widely understood that the 'Keynesean settlement' began to unravel at a policy level with the election of the Fraser Government in 1975 (Campbell and Sherrington, 2006: 98-99), the homogenous massification of schooling has endured as the dominant narrative, long after it has been irrevocably displaced by the rise of the non-government schooling sector, the exponential rise of the social and actual wage, and long after the originally conceived benchmarks of basic attainment and equitable access have been reached. In other words, ITE students are often being trained to fit into an outdated narrative that no longer describes society or the schools markets in which they will be employed, or, at worst, experiencing non-purposefully fragmented arrays of various conflicting narratives, through a sequence of disconnected units and practicums, effectively graduating with no unifying meta-story of what it means to teach.

Challenge 5: Attrition in initial teacher education.

Another challenge in contemporary Australian teacher workforce planning, is the unsustainably high rates of attrition, both in training and in the first five years of teaching. This is problematic for a number of reasons, but for the purposes of this paper, our main concern is an unstable and unpredictable staffing situation. (Gallant and Riley, 2014; Kearney, 2014; Weldon, 2018).

AITSL notes that the average completion rate for Bachelor's level ITE is 56%.

The six year completion rate for ITE students who commenced in 2010 was 56% (n=11,140) for undergraduates and 79% (n=6,810) for postgraduates……Both ITE undergraduates and postgraduates have experienced an 8% decline in six year completion rates between the 2005 and 2010 commencing cohorts. This decline is steeper compared to that of other higher education programs. (Institute for Teaching and School Leadership, 2017: 54, xiv)

What is not measured in AITSL's figures, and as far as I know remains as yet unmeasured, is the impact of the *first practicum* on in-course ITE attrition. This typically occurs in the first half of the second year, and so postdates AITSL's measurement point. Measuring this would constitute crucial data for the assessment of different modes of professional placement, which will be discussed at a later point in this paper. What is even more disturbing is the high rates of early career attrition, which some research places as high as 50% in first five years of teaching (Kearney, 2014). Even at a conservative measure, it is likely that only 30-35% of students who start a teaching degree, will still be teaching after five years. Indeed, According to Miles and Knipe, 'Beginning teachers suffer from 'transition shock' as they move from teaching programs into employment as a teacher.' (2018; Goddard, O'Brien and Goddard, 2013).)

Yet despite the attrition out of ITE programmes, there appears in fact to be an over-supply of new beginning teachers in Melbourne and Sydney, and a radical undersupply in most other locations And yet this over-supply does not appear to be driving up choice in teacher quality for school principals in capital cities (Patty, 2014).

These high rates of attrition suggest three negative trends. Firstly that Australian ITE is widely attracting the wrong kinds of candidates, secondly that it is training them in unsuccessful ways and thirdly, that there is a significant dislocation between ITE preparation and actual industry needs in schools.

Challenge 6: The mass retail model of Australian ITE.

These relate to a deeper systemic cause: that the two key metrics driving much of Australian tertiary are not conducive to guaranteeing high-quality teacher training.

The first key metric for most tertiary providers is what might be depicted as a 'retail' provider-centred relationship between tertiary and an individual student, who pays the university for a fixed product- a course of study. The tertiary provider determines who is enrolled, how they are trained, course content, practicum experience, and significantly influences an individual teacher's accreditation.

A second key metric is research output- attracting Excellence in Research Australia (ERA) points, which in turn, attracts institutional status and government funding.

The second key metric is fed by the first key metric: increased student enrolments, leads to increased funding for research, research output enhances status and more government funding, and higher status, attracts higher enrolments. And so the cycle continues. Given the essential, high volume role of school education, ITE represents a guaranteed student enrolment market, or, as Professor Steve

Dinham put it, a 'cash cow' (Patty, 2014). Australian public universities- and the handful of private ones- stand to gain if they lower entrance requirements to attract large volumes of ITE students.

Indeed, depending on calculation method, the average ATAR into ITE in the last 10 years has been less than 70 (Institute for Teaching Standards and Leadership, 2017: xii). In addition, most selection processes in universities do not account for the emotional and personable requirements that contribute to the success of teaching: proven volunteerism, a sense of deep altruism, team readiness, and a love of community connection (TEMAG, 2014: xv, xviii, 13). A good ATAR alone, will not a successful teacher make.

Given these systemic distractions, it is reasonable to claim that the actual needs of the school industry: i.e. classroom-ready, high quality teaching graduates, clearly aligned to the needs of school end-users- are not the key metrics driving contemporary Australian ITE courses. Unlike medicine, or surveying, or accounting, or most other professions, the Australian teaching industry has no authoritative 'college' of practitioners that speaks authoritatively back into the training of teachers[11]. There are few mechanisms to facilitate dialogue, between tertiary and school. The dominant ITE model is provider-oriented, not industry-oriented. In general, tertiary is not sufficiently supplying teachers for the areas that have highest demand, and is over-supplying areas with lowest demand.

According to Professor Steve Dinham:

> *The current practice whereby universities are free to enrol students in teacher education courses until they fill course quotas, regardless of academic ability, clearly needs to be reviewed.* (Dinham, 2013: 16-17)

---

[11] The voluntary, collegiate bodies of *Australian College of Education* and *Australian College of Education Leadership* do not have any mandated authority.

Challenge 7: The massive economic waste in Australian teacher training.

Almost all of these teaching places are Commonwealth Supported Places (CSPs). Based on annual expenditure on ITE CSPs, the current attrition rates cost well over $300 million of wasted CSP money annually This increases to over $400 million annual loss of public money if factoring in the cost of early-career staff churn. (Kearney, 2014; Hastie, Hutchinson and Jensen, 2018). [12]

And yet there is no evidence of this wastage being recorded as a line item in federal or state budgets, school systems or schools. Nor is the immense and draining cost of performance-managing poor staff in schools. Both appear to be merely written off as the cost of doing business.

Challenge 8: Disconnection of tertiary education faculties from schools.

Under most current arrangements, education faculties training teachers, cannot be structurally held accountable for course or career attrition. In this scenario, a course could be over theoretical, with content demonstrably irrelevant to teaching – a common caricature, and one perhaps not entirely undeserved. It is a perception amongst many that many university education departments tend to hold a politically monolithic position- typically politically progressive, anti-religious, and anti-non-government schooling (Donnelly, 2018). Such caricatures are unfair to many hard-working and even-handed education academics, yet I would argue that it is nonetheless reasonable to suggest that the current systemic arrangements are likely to cultivate

---

[12] In rough terms, this would equate to the cost of building 14 new schools annually. According the NSW Department of Planning, around 150 new schools will be required over the next ten years. Much of this cost could be recouped if teacher attrition was significantly reduced. And so on.

a culture of disconnection between education academics and school end-users of ITE graduates.

The apex of contemporary ITE clinical practice models

This paper has raised eight challenges to HR supply in Australian Christian-affiliated schools. In future papers, it will be demonstrated that various solutions to these problems are being operated through a variety of clinical teaching partnerships in variety of places, both domestically and internationally. However I will also argue that these are less holistic than needed, and propose that an apex combination of existing approaches exists in an integrated workplace training model manifested in the partnership between Alphacrucis College and St Phillip's Christian School *Teaching School* model in the NSW Hunter (St Philip's Teaching School, 2021), The Teaching School Alliance Sydney (TSAS, 2021), and the St Thomas Aquinas Teaching School in Tasmania (St Thomas Aquinas teaching schools institute, 2021). In the 2021 NSW Budget, 2.9 million was allocated for a pilot study into the model (Alphacrucis College, 2021) and the 2021 *Quality initial teacher education review* (Australian government department of education skills and employment, 2021) is taking submissions as this paper is being written. The author and the Alphacrucis team were called as witnesses to the inquiry, and the model is attracting the positive attention of legislators and educators in a range of contexts. It remains to be seen if the model can alleviate the challenges facing Australian teacher formation at large scale, but at a small scale appears to be a direct solution.

Works cited

ABS. (2019). Table 42b. Number of full time and part time students. 2006-2018. 4221.0 - Schools, Australia, 2018. Australian Bureau of Statistics.

https://www.abs.gov.au/AUSSTATS/abs@.nsf/DetailsPage/4221.02018?OpenDocument

Alphacrucis College. (2019). Graduate attributes. Alphacrucis College. https://www.ac.edu.au/graduate-attributes/

Alphacrucis College. (2021). Hub model- NSW budget announcement. Alphacrucis College. https://www.ac.edu.au/news-community/media-releases/hub-model-nsw-budget-announcement/

Australian Broadcasting Corporation. (2013, July 7). Alex Greenwich 'appalled' by loophole allowing private schools to expel gay students. ABC News. http://www.abc.net.au/news/

Australian government department of education skills and employment. (2021). Quality initial teacher education review. https://www.dese.gov.au/quality-initial-teacher-education-review

Bourdieu, P. (1992). Language & symbolic Power. Cambridge, Massachusetts Harvard University Press

Bourdieu, P. (1986). 'The forms of capital'. In Richardson (Ed.) Handbook of theory and research for the sociology of education (241-258). New York. Greenwood Press

Browne, R. (2015, May 6). Scripture classes: Calls for crackdown on public schools. Sydney Morning Herald. https://www.smh.com.au/

Campbell, A., McNamara, O., Furlong, J., Lewis, S., & Howson, J. (2008). The Evaluation of the National Partnership Project in England: Processes, issues and dilemmas in commissioned evaluation research. Journal of Education for Teaching, 33(4), 471-483

Campbell, C. and Sherrington, G. (2006). The comprehensive public high school. Historical perspectives. New York. Palgrave Macmillan

Caro, J and Bonner, C. Stupid Country: How Australia is Dismantling Public Education. Sydney, NSW, Australia University of New South Wales Press

Carson, D. (2015). A critical analysis of Teen sex by the book. Fairness of Religion in Schools (FIRIS). http://religionsinschool.com/wp-content/uploads/2015/05/Carson-2015-Review-Teen-Sex-by-the-Book.pdf

CDF. (1985). 'Nota explicativa alla notificazione sulle opere di P. Jon Sobrino, S.I.'. Congregation for the Doctrine of the Faith. http://212.77.1.245/news_services/bulletin/news/19857.php?index=19857&lang=po#TRADUZIONE%20IN%20LINGUA%20%20INGLESE

CEN. (2019). Transformation by design. Christian Education National https://www.estore.nice.edu.au/collections/featured/products/transformation-by-design-crafting-formational-learning

Cox, L. (2013, October 19). Gay students say school tried to correct them. Canberra Times. http://www.canberratimes.com.au[A1]/

Credit Suisse. (2018). Global wealth report. 18 October. https://www.credit-suisse.com/about-us-news/en/articles/news-and-expertise/global-wealth-report-2018-us-and-china-in-the-lead-201810.html

CSA. (2019). Locating learners in God's big story. Christian Schools Australia. https://csa.edu.au/resources/curriculum-resources/

Dinham, S. (2013). Connecting clinical teaching to instructional leadership. Australian Journal of Education 57(3) 225–236

Donnelly, K. (2018). Wisdom, truth give way as left conformity prevails. The Australian. https://www.theaustralian.com.au/commentary/opinion/wisdom-truth-give-way-as-left-conformity-prevails/news-story/501e0637875f183bacb75880c97431cc

Edcomm. (2019). Home page. https://www.edcomm.org.au/

Etzioni, A. (1996). The responsive community: A communitarian perspective. American Sociological Review, 61, 9

Foucault, M. (1977). Discipline and Punish: The Birth of the Prison. Translated by Alan Sheridan, London: Allen Lane, Penguin

Foucault, M. (2002). The archaeology of knowledge. Oxon: Routledge

Fukuyama, F. (1995). Trust: The social virtues and the creation of prosperity. New York: Free Press. p. 26

Fullan, M. (2004). Leading in a culture of change. San Francisco. Jossey-Bass

Gal, S. and Brueck, H. (2018). The wealthy country. Australians are the richest people in the world. The Sydney Morning Herald. 9 November. https://www.smh.com.au/business/the-economy/the-wealthy-country-australians-are-the-richest-people-in-the-world-20181109-p50eyc.html

Gallant, A., & Riley, P. (2014). Early career teacher attrition: new thoughts on an intractable problem. Teacher Development 18.4 (August), pp.1-19

Goddard, R., O'Brien, P. & Goddard, M. (2013). Work environment predictors of beginning teacher burnout. British Education Research Journal. 32, 6. pp. 857-874

Greenwich, A. (2013a). Ending discrimination in private schools: Discussion paper. Alex Greenwich latest news. http://www.alexgreenwich.com/ada

Greenwich, A. (2013b, October 1). Letters from gay students. How our schools tried to fix us. News.com.au. https://www.news.com.au/

Hastie, D. (2019). Live interview between author and news anchor Ros Bird. ABC news 24. March 28. Australian Broadcasting Authority. https://www.youtube.com/watch?v=CknugEo_ITE

Hastie, D. (2018a). Should we ban books in schools? Arguments from the public history of Australian school text censorship. English in Australia, 53 (3)

Hastie, D. (2018b) Labor risks voter whirlwind with attack on faith-based schools. Sydney Morning Herald. 6 December https://www.smh.com.au/politics/federal/labor-risks-voter-whirlwind-with-attack-on-faith-based-schools-20181205-p50ke7.html

Hastie, D. (2017). The latest instalment in the Whig interpretation of Australian education history: Catherine Byrne's JORH article 'Free, compulsory and (not) secular'. Journal of Religious History. Vol 41 (3). September 2017. pp. 386-403

Hastie, D. (2010). The retreat from Critical Literacy in the new Australian English Curriculum. Journal of Christian Education (JCE), 53, (1). September 1, 2011

Hastie, D. (2012). In Search of Holy Transcripts: Approaches to Researching Religious Schools. Journal of Education and Christian Belief, 16(1), pp. 41–59

Hastie, D., Hutchinson, M. & Jensen, N. (2018). Alphacrucis College submission to the Inquiry into the status of the teaching profession. Commonwealth House of Representatives Standing Committee on Employment, Education and Training. Sydney. Alphacrucis College

Institute for Teaching and School Leadership. (2017). Initial teacher education: data report 2017, AITSL, Melbourne. https://www.aitsl.edu.au/tools-resources/resource/initial-teacher-education-data-report-2017

Institute for Teaching and School Leadership. (2011). Accreditation of Initial Teacher Education Programs in Australia – Standards and Procedures. http://pandora.nla.gov.au/pan/146149/20160516-0129/www.aitsl.edu.au/docs/default-source/aitslresearch/insights/re00004_accreditation_of_initial_teacher_education_programs_in_australia_standards_and_procedures_apr_20115014.pdf

ISCA. (2018). Snapshot. Independent Schools Council of Australia. https://isca.edu.au/snapshot-2018/

Kearney, S. (2019). Conversation between author and Associate Professor Sean Kearney, Associate Dean, School of Education, Notre Dame University Sydney. 22 February 2019

Kearney, S. (2014). Teacher attrition, retention and mobility: Where & Society, 32(2), 5-24

Legal and Constitutional Affairs References Committee. (2018). Legislative exemptions that allow faith-based educational institutions to discriminate against students, teachers and staff, Report.
https://www.aph.gov.au/Parliamentary_Business/Committees/Senate/Legal_and_Constitutional_Affairs/Schooldiscrimination/Report

Maddox, M. (2013). Letter to Tim Heasley. Chair Fairness In Religion In Schools. Friday 12 April 2013 http://religionsinschool.com/wp-content/uploads/2011/02/Maddox-Review-of-CRE_final1.pdf

Maddox, M. (2014b). Rise of private schools marks return to 19th century wast. Op Ed. The Age. February 8, 2014 http://www.theage.com.au/comment/rise-of-private-schools-marks-return-to-19th-century-waste-20140207-32745.html

Maddox, M. (2014c). Too Much Faith in Schools: The Rise of Christian Schooling in Australia. ABC Religion and Ethics Online 20 Mar 2014
http://www.abc.net.au/religion/articles/2014/03/20/3968199.htm

Maddox, M. (2014d). Sprawling Divisions: A Reply to David Hastie. ABC Religion and Ethics Online 28 Apr 2014
http://www.abc.net.au/religion/articles/2014/04/28/3993631.htm

Maddox, M. (2014e). School chaplains' challenge reveals Australia's weak religious freedoms. The Guardian.
http://www.theguardian.com/commentisfree/2014/may/

08/school-chaplains-challenge-reveals-australias-weak-religious-freedoms

Maddox, M. (2014f). Chaplaincy programme has no place in state schools. Op Ed. Sydney Morning Herald. June 19 http://www.smh.com.au/comment/chaplaincy-program-has-no-place-in-state-schools-20140619-zsen7.html

Maddox, M. (2014a). Taking God to School. The end of Australia's egalitarian education? Sydney. Allen & Unwin.

Maddox, M. & O'Doherty, S. (2014g). Religious-schools: are they undermining egalitarian education? Radio broadcast. Religion and Ethics Report. ABC Radio National. 12 February http://www.abc.net.au/radionational/programs/religionandethicsreport/religious-schools3a-are-they-undermining-egalitarian-education/5255362

McIlroy, T. (2013, May 26). Public sector better for gay students: Kirby. Sydney Morning Herald. https://www.smh.com.au/

Miles, R., & Knipe, S. (2018). 'I sorta felt like I was out in the middle of the ocean': Novice teachers' transition to the classroom. Australian Journal of Teacher Education, 43(6)

Mohammed, A. (2009). Transforming School Culture: How to Overcome Staff Division (Leadership Strategies to Build a Professional Learning Community). Bloomington IND. Solution Tree Press

Munro, K. (2017). Ethics classes in NSW primary schools growing despite barriers to enrolment. The Sydney Morning Herald. 27 January. https://www.smh.com.au/education/ethics-classes-in-nsw-primary-schools-growing-despite-barriers-to-enrolment-20170124-gtxppa.html

Musset, P. (2012), 'School choice and equity: Current policies in OECD countries and a literature review', OECD Education Working Papers, No. 66, OECD Publishing. http://dx.doi.org/10.1787/5k9fq23507vc-en

NICE. (2019). Courses. National Institute of Christian Education. https://www.nice.edu.au/academics/post-graduate-courses

Ongley, H. (2015). This horrific sex ed book is teaching girls to fear gay people and short skirts. Xojane Website. http://www.xojane.com/issues/this-horrific-sex-ed-book-is-teaching-girls-to-fear-gay-people-and-short-skirts

Onyx, J and Bullen, P. (2000). Measuring social capital in five communities. Journal of applied behavioural science. 23-46

O'Shea, G. (2018). Telephone conversation between the author and Dr Gerard O'Shea, Assistant Director of Catholic Education in Mission and Religious Education, Wilcannia-Forbes Catholic Education Office. 20 June 2019

Parliament of Australia. (2018a). Legislative exemptions that allow faith-based educational institutions to discriminate against students, teachers and staff. SENATE STANDING COMMITTEES ON LEGAL AND CONSTITUTIONAL AFFAIRS. https://www.aph.gov.au/Parliamentary_Business/Committees/Senate/Legal_and_Constitutional_Affairs/Schooldiscrimination

Parliament of Australia. (2018b). Sex discrimination amendment (removing discrimination against students). https://www.aph.gov.au/Parliamentary_Business/Bills_LEGislation/Bills_Search_Results/Result?bId=s1162

Patty, A. (2014). Graduate glut puts trainee teachers on the scrapheap. The Sydney Morning Herald. 20 October. https://www.smh.com.au/education/graduate-glut-puts-trainee-teachers-on-the-scrapheap-20141019-115wa4.html

Piggin, S. and Linder, R.D. (2018). The fountain of public prosperity. Evangelical Christians in Australian History, 1740-1910. Melbourne. Monash University Press.

Putnam, R. (1995). Tuning in, tuning out: The strange disappearance of social capital in America. The 1995 Ithiel de Sola Pool Lecture. Political Science and Politics, pp. 664-683

St Andrew's Cathedral School. (2019). Learning in the heart of the City. St Andrew's Cathedral School home page. https://www.sacs.nsw.edu.au/

St Philip's Teaching School. (2018). St Philip's Christian College. Offering a uniquely better approach to teacher training. Newcastle. St Philip's Teaching School Hub. https://www.flipsnack.com/teachingschoolbrochure/st-philip-s-teaching-school-brochure.html

Staff in Australian Schools 2013 main report. (2013). Staff in Australian Schools (SIAS) 2013 main report. Australian Council for Education Research. Commonwealth of Australia. https://docs.education.gov.au/system/files/doc/other/sias_2013_main_report.pdf

St Therese's. (2019). Welcome. Catholic Education Office of the Diocese of Wilcannia - Forbeshttp://www.wf.catholic.edu.au/find-a-school/st-thereses-community-school-wilcannia/

St Thomas Aquinas teaching schools institute. (2021). Home page. https://catholic.tas.edu.au/teaching-schools

Sydney Boys High. (2019). Army cadets. Co-curricular programmes. Sydney Boys High. http://www.sydneyboyshigh.com/curriculum/cocurricular

Symes, C., and McIntyre, J. (2000). Working knowledge: The new Vocationalism and higher education. PA. Open University Press

TEMAG. (2014). Action now. Classroom ready teachers. Teacher Education Ministerial Advisory Group https://docs.education.gov.au/system/files/doc/other/action_now_classroom_ready_teachers_print.pdf

TEQSA. (2019). Providers. Web page. https://www.teqsa.gov.au/

TSAS (2021). Home page. Teaching school alliance Sydney. https://www.teachingschoolsalliancesydney.org/

Weldon, P. (2018). Early career teacher attrition in Australia: evidence, definition, classification and measurement. Australian Journal of Education 62.1 (April), pp.61-78

Wood, A. (2015a, May 9). Anglican Church angry over Department of Education banning of 'one-partner' material. The Daily Telegraph. https://www.dailytelegraph.com.au/

Wood, A. (2015b, May 20). Banned books back in classroom after Department of Education backs down. The Daily Telegraph. htp://www.dailytelegraph.com.au/

Yan Jiang, J. and Lieu, C.W. (2014). High performance work systems and organizational effectiveness: The mediating role of social capital. Human Resource Management Review. 25(1) November 2014

FAITH AND FAMILY: THE FUNDAMENTAL PRINCIPLES OF AN EDUCATED NATION

Cheryl Lacey

On the 8 December 1986 my brother pointed a gun at his head and pulled the trigger.

The handwritten note he had left in the kitchen of his rented property was an apology for being a burden to our family.

His final words couldn't be further from the truth.

To reconcile the completed suicide of a 25-year-old man lies firmly within the context of faith and family.

In this colloquium we've been invited to explore one fundamental question:

How can parents, the primary educators of children, work effectively with schools to make Christ real for their children?

This question has been explored and debated through historical contexts, statistics, research, opinion, pedagogy, and philosophy. I too will be relying on some of these contexts. However, if we're serious about effecting change, because of the exploration of this most important question, we must be prepared to replace numbers with names, research with lived experience and above all else, replace apologies with compassionate action.

My brother's life and death are central to this question, that I too have been asking for 35 years. And, while so many of those questions will forever remain unanswered, so many answers have come from the most extraordinary people in the most unexpected of circumstances. I couldn't be more grateful.

It is impossible to speak to the answers without weaving the unanswered questions of my brother's life and death in Melbourne - into this curious tapestry of parents, faith, and school.

Today I'll be sharing five fundamental principles, which I believe are the essential foundations of genuine Australian school education. They place family firmly in the centre. To embrace them, in my view, is to ensure an acceptance of Christian faith for all Australian families, through home and school education, whether there is a belief in Christ or not.

These five principles are:
- The language of agreement
- Australian schools not schools in Australia
- Diverse Ability – The Dignified Currency
- The matter of law for leaders and learners
- Education has purpose meaning and impact

Principle 1: The language of agreement

We all have our own unique vocabulary that is rich with words that have evolved overtime, take for example the word chair. It comes from the Greek word *kathedra* via the Latin *cathedra*, and the French *chaire*, which means the Bishop's seat or throne. Over time with the regular use of chair became a term used to reference other seats beyond the church, while in English cathedra evolved into cathedral, the seat of a Bishop's power. Today when we hear the word chair, we might not picture the original concept of a throne, but we certainly wouldn't picture a stool or a bench.

The concept of family has also evolved over time. For decades it was widely accepted that a family was a nuclear group consisting of mum, dad, and their offspring. Today, there are many recognised family structures. Take mine for example. If it wasn't for two pairs of biological parents, one from Hong Kong and one from Thailand, I wouldn't be a mother. I adopted my two extraordinary daughters.

Three more concepts that effect our life and indeed - for life - are schools, schooling, and education. These concepts are often used interchangeably, however the distinction between them is one of great importance.

Melbourne's first public building was constructed in 1837, the cost of which was met by donations from citizens of various denominations. It was used for services on Sabbath and Sundays and as a school during the week. Several decades later, during the gold rush, tents were used as schools and places of general worship.

It could be argued that the genuine purpose of education – to change people through teaching - was the very ideal our early settlers pursued. Limited resources and lack of personal wealth were no barrier to their intent.

On the contrary, I like to believe the intent was to bring families together 'in good faith'.

The benefit to growing communities was the introduction of schooling to those families, familiar with faith, but inadequately abreast of the value and possibilities school education could provide.

How blessed we are to learn from this historical context, for the language of ideas and concepts are the true power behind progress, innovation, and civil society. They provide us with genuine platforms for robust debate, research, and investment.

Since the beginning of this century, schools have focussed on what is referred as 21st century skills. Tens of millions of dollars have been spent on professional development to achieve this target. The common theme is the search for a 'common language.'

To stop here, as most schools have done, is to fail to identify the genesis of ideas and concepts, and how words form meaning, but, like the chair, agreement on how meanings are applied must follow.

When a language of agreement is honoured, the meaning of family is not confused with gender; equality is not confused with entitlement; fairness is not confused with cultural heritage; parent is not confused with government; and most importantly 'in good faith' is not confused with religion.

Principle 2: Australian Schools NOT Schools in Australia

The capacity to recognise a distinction, or to differentiate, is a remarkable innate trait without which we could not survive.

Babies are hard-wired to discriminate – to identify their mothers' features among those of other women. We discriminate between edible plants and toxic species to avoid poisoning. We discriminate between the features, traits, and behaviours of prospective partners, so as to find love.

Despite its value, discrimination has come to be considered as the modern taboo, in what amounts to a contempt for our personal beliefs and qualities, and those we share. Its ultimate targets are history and religion.

Consider the following statements:

Can you discriminate between those that are factual, those that are false or incorrect, and those that represent belief or opinion?

1. There is only one god.
2. All women are pure.
3. Queen Elizabeth I established the Church of England.
4. All men of the cloth are paedophiles.
5. There are many gods.

Schools actively teach discrimination using a strategy known as 'comparing and contrasting', for instance, comparing and contrasting a character's traits at the beginning of a novel with those at the end.

But schools also discriminate between materials in recommended texts and print media that compromise the accurate teaching of religious and historical content. Spending on the consequences of these poor choices, has become a viable solution – one that must cease.

We must have faith in robust debate that distinguishes between truth and fabrication. And that must begin with an appreciation of how and why the relationship between parents and schools has evolved.

Prior to Federation, New South Wales introduced a national education system, a system inherited by Victoria. At the same time, land distribution, diversity in population, and financial support for some denominations over others were of great concern. Financial and religious positions determined access to education.

Political and religious battles began. The loss of trust resulted in a major fallout between government, parents, and faith groups. A centralised public system was born, and the Public Education Act of 1876 was passed.

Local control of schools, once shared by families and the community, was removed and financial aid to church-based schools abolished. It was the beginning of government control over schools, the purpose of which was to provide free, compulsory, and secular education.

However, we must appreciate that secular education was intended to provide fundamental teachings in core areas including English and Mathematics, without the influence of any one overriding Christian influence.

Australia's first census, held in 1911, provides some relevance to the possible intentions behind this more centralised approach to schooling. This 1911 census identified that among Australia's 4.5 million residents, a total of 357 religious categories were acknowledged.

And given that the National Education in the colony of Victoria had devolved power to communities, with a firm undertaking that any school must maintain Christianity as an intrinsic value, it could be argued that secular education was never intended to ignore religion or faith, but rather to tackle the issue of land distribution for schools between different denominations. And we must not forget that early schooling was dominated by the social, and moral needs of our early immigrants.

Today Australia still claims to be a religiously diverse nation. Yet, the 2016 census indicated that only three religious categories were of significant influence – Christianity (52%), Islam (2.6%) and Buddhism (2.4%). 30% of Australians reported that they have no religion. Is this the same as saying 30% of Australia's population has no moral principles? I don't believe this to be so. However, this comparison between the 2016 census and that of 1911, clearly indicates faith, spiritual loyalty and freedom has gradually fallen into decline.

In the first principle I identified the need for a language of agreement. And it's here where we find ourselves once more.

What does secular currently mean in the context of school education?

When society permits halal certification and the wearing of Islamic headscarves, or acknowledges Christmas Day and Yom Kippur, is that consistent with a 'secular' Australia?

Does the complete removal of God and religion from the public sphere mean a total separation of church and state? Is secularism a dilution of religious belief and practice – as in the maintaining of marriage, but with the relinquishment of its true meaning? Or is it a blending of many religious beliefs, including Islam and atheism?

In other words, can Australia be a religiously plural nation? And can we trust schools to honour the final agreement?

Our way of life, and indeed our Constitution, are enshrined in the religious beliefs and practices of Judeo-Christian foundations. We must have a language of agreement regarding these ideas, values, and principles.

An agreed definition of 'secular' can ensure every Australian school is underpinned by these values rather than schools in Australia becoming religious entities and conflicting moral high grounds of their own.

Principle 3: Diverse Ability – the dignified currency

Everyone has the ability or the means to do something. Over the course of a lifetime we acquire additional abilities, and our existing abilities might change. Many develop and improve, some remain the same, and others decline or become less effective. We all have diverse ability.

In schools, teachers regularly attempt to adapt or adjust the curriculum and their practice to accommodate their own, and their students', different abilities.

Parents are also adjusting and accommodating the different abilities of their children, including talents and interests, biological differences, and birth order.

Making adjustments is a natural part of the learning and teaching process and it is a natural part of parenting.

Awareness of difference was also a natural and expected feature of early school education.

Scholarships were available for individuals who displayed competencies, capabilities, and interest in further learning. Citizens as young as 14 were able to attend university. Some acquired multiple degrees, in areas including engineering, chemistry and law. Many used their education to contribute to the building of our great nation.

Over time difference became increasingly focused on disability. Children living with disability were either ignored or segregated; they certainly couldn't attend mainstream schools. That was until the 1980s, when integration was introduced into public policy. This gave children with a disability the right to be enrolled in a mainstream school – now referred to as inclusion.

For some parents whose children have a disability, inclusion has been a tremendous success. For others, it is has come at a great cost. The introduction of the National Disability Standards for Education have been developed to ensure all children of compulsory school age, including those living with a disability, have the same educational opportunities and choices, including the right to attend a mainstream school.

And herein lies the problem.

These disability standards focus on a synergy between the provider of state education and the recognised disability of the student. These standards do not honour the right of the parent and their relationship or contribution to their own child's education. Home-schooling, while possible, is not afforded the same assistance.

A focus on disability also means other students are ignored, including those with a gift or talent. And we must also be cognizant that compulsory school attendance concludes often before young adults with recognised disabilities obtain the necessary capabilities for future work and life.

For parents to have faith in a school system, governments must have faith in parents. Disability must not be used to invite parents to accept state schooling as the only form of necessary education. If the term disability were replaced with the term diverse ability and there was a language of agreement about its meaning, Judeo Christian values, on which Australian schools should be founded, would be honoured in word and deed.

Principle 4: The matter of law for learners and leaders

Schools operate within a complex web of Federal and State laws that have an impact on the rights and responsibilities of school leaders, students, teachers, parents, and others connected to school-based education.

The many legal issues in schools include, but are not limited to, professional conduct, student injury, child custody matters, the right to religious freedom and mandatory reporting. All require an understanding of the law.

Prior to the introduction of constitutional law, Victoria's Education Act 1872 was simple in its explanation for the purpose of free, compulsory, and secular education, the role of teachers and a standard curriculum. It also included the use of school buildings, scholarships beyond the standard curriculum and the requirements to obtain a certificate declaring a *child being sufficiently educated*. It is 6 pages long, and a fascinating read. Today, Victoria's Training and Reform Act, 2006 (version 75) is 791 pages long.

In less than 150 years, Victorian Education has shifted from a doctrine of optimism, where faith and schooling resided under one community roof, to a legal quagmire.

Its original purpose and its commitment to a free education for every child, and for every parent be assured financial support if necessary, have been strangled by an obsession for more legislation. Respect for our moral footprint has all but vanished. And upon further investigation, despite the complexity that the law brings to education, there is no reference to school education in the Victorian constitution nor the Australian constitution.

Two questions we must ask ourselves are these:
1   What is the relationship between Canon law, state schooling, education, and Australia's Constitution?
2   What is the relationship between parent and child in relation to schools, schooling education and faith?

Another question: Could it be that the omission of school education in Australia's constitution provides the catalyst for the introduction of competition to inject genuine rights and responsibilities of parents regarding their children's education?

If nothing else, debate over school competition would require a language of agreement to be reached, for any further inquiry and consideration of potential pathways, for parents to be positioned firmly, in the centre of the life and faith of their children.

Principle 5: Education has purpose, meaning and impact

For centuries philosophers have sought answers to the purpose of education and have also asked what it means to have a good education and how education relates to life and life's purposes.

Some believe education should prepare us to enter the workforce. Others believe the purpose of education should be focused more on social, academic, cultural, and intellectual development. We could then think critically, and debate with authority on issues of importance.

There is no right or wrong answer.

Put simply, the purpose of education is to change people through teaching. The change involves learning or moving from not knowing to knowing. And, because learning is such a personal process, education has a different value and purpose for each of us.

Most of us understand that learning happens continuously, over the course of a lifetime, as each individual think, and feels and acts. The phrase lifelong learning signifies this understanding.

As a young, growing, and dynamic nation, a view was put forward that every child should be afforded the chance to reach an agreed standard of competency in reading, writing and arithmetic. Parental income, religion and social status should never be reasons for the denial of a child's right to achieve this agreed standard.

Free, compulsory, and secular school education would be provided for every child aged 6-15 years. Not more than four hours per day, over 120 days per calendar year, would be allocated for this instruction.

If children demonstrated the aptitude and enthusiasm for further learning, parents could pay teachers – as they would a tutor – for further study. A standard education, combined with the opportunity for further study would benefit the child, the family, and the growing colony. It was the best of all possible worlds.

Today, school enrolment is compulsory. The years of expected attendance have expanded, the curriculum is overloaded, and school-based teachers are no longer chosen, nor paid, by parents. Faith has all but disappeared in government school education.

There is a way forward.

It begins with a language of agreement, on a national standard of education in English, Mathematics, studies in Western Civilisation and Health available in every Australian school for every Australian citizen. Diverse ability would evolve over the course of an entire lifetime in places within and beyond the school gate.

The matter of law would be simplified by clear statements of intent at federal, state, and regional level. A synergy of difference between church and state would be inclusive of the role and responsibility of parents in the life and education of their children.

In 1986 my brother completed suicide. He attended free compulsory and secular education, had religious instruction in primary school and attended Sunday school.

For 35 years his life and death have underpinned this journey of discovery about the value and purpose of school, schooling, and education. More importantly, it has shone a light on faith and family and the possibility that these two elements become the driving force for Australian schools to become everything our founding fathers imagined.

He was never a burden. God bless him.

WHO ARE THE ADOLESCENTS TODAY?

Eamonn Pollard

Today I am going to talk about what I think some of qualities of a good Religious Education practitioner are, some of the realities that many of the teenagers in our schools are facing today, the historical currents which have got us to this point and an alternative narrative which can support teenagers live lives of meaning and maybe faith. This is a very ambitious scope for the time I have, so it will be a brief commentary on each of the topics I have mentioned.

The twentieth century educational philosopher Peters wisely stated 'to be educated is not to have arrived at a destination; it is to travel with a different view.'[1] One of the explicit hopes of Catholic education is that graduates of Catholic education travel with a Christian worldview, illuminated by faith. How is this achieved?

I would like to start by referencing a painting by Holman Hunt which was painted in the 1850s called *The Light of the World*. You have no doubt seen it before. There is Jesus with a lamp at knocking at a door. I think the key part of the picture is that if you look closely, the door has no handle. The point as I see it? Jesus is always knocking at the door, but it is up to us to open the door. I think that a relationship

---

[1] R. S. Peters, Education as initiation. Inaugural lecture, *Institute of Education, University of London*, London, 9 December, 1963.

with the risen Christ is always open from Jesus' side and not always open from our side. I have felt for many years that this is particularly relevant to the spirituality of teenagers. The question is, how do we encourage teenagers to open the door?

I think a large part of the success or otherwise of Catholic education comes down to who is teaching it. A lot of what I am going to suggest today about the faith life is that encounter is a large part of it and that in a school context, the staff are central to this. We who work in schools have the task of seeing the face of Christ in our students and to be the face of Christ to our students.

Very briefly, I think there are four features we are looking for in our religious educators:

1. We need people of faith.
2. We need people with some theological and scriptural formation.
3. We need good pedagogical practitioners.
4. We need more than solid content.

A good religious education educates the head, heart and hands. It is not limited to academic Religious Education, but we also need to be including prayer and reflection, retreats and a liturgical life, to educate the heart. Outreach in service to others also needs to be part of a good Catholic education.

At the heart of what I believe about the faith formation of teenagers is that it is ultimately about the opportunity for an encounter with the risen, living Christ. It is part of our birthright to experience the incarnational God. Reflective opportunities draw out the inner life experience and Religious Education gives us the language to express the internal workings of the spirit. The door to the faith life might open.

As important as the curriculum and the teachers are, I think we need to start with the students. Spiritual and religious formation is not something that we do to students but do with. We need to understand and know our students, care for them and want what is best for them. So who are our teenagers today and what is it like to be a teenager today?

While in many ways, today's teenagers have it pretty good, the sad news is that we have an epidemic of teenager anxiety and depression. What is worse is that the leading cause of death amongst 15–24-year-olds is suicide. I think the hardest thing I have done in a school context is to tell students and staff of the suicide of a girl in Year 9 a few years ago.

Here are some statistics for teenagers that are mostly from the last five to ten years.

Mission Australia's 2017 annual Youth Survey had mental health as the number one national concern, for the first time in their 16 years of undertaking the surveys. The Royal Society for Public Health claims that rates of anxiety and depression for young people have increased by 70% in the last 25 years.[2] Tomyn has studied subjective wellbeing for Australians across the life cycle and concluded that the ages of 15-16 are the most challenging in the life cycle.[3] Headspace have released data showing that 32% of 12-25 year-old young Australians are 'reporting high or very high levels of psychological distress.'[4] In 2009 the figure was 9%, so the proportion of students reporting psychological distress according to Headspace's data, has more than tripled in less than 10 years.

Another alarming statistic from *The Medical Journal of Australia* is that young people between the ages of 10 and 19 receiving treatment for 'suicidal urges, self-harm or intentional poisoning' increased by 159% between 2010 and

---

[2] The Royal Society for Public Health, *#StatusofMind.*, 2015, para. 9.
[3] A. Tomyn, *Youth Connections Subjective Wellbeing Report*, 2014.
[4] Headspace, *New headspace research reveals alarming levels of psychological distress in young Australians*, 2018, para 2.

2014.[5] Mission Australia have noted that if you are a teenager, you are more likely to have a mental illness.[6]

This is who we are working with when we talk about students in High Schools. This is the reality that teachers are dealing with. We spend far more time these days on teenager wellbeing issues than behaviour issues. We have a significant problem and the strategies we are using are no doubt mitigating, but we have a long way to go. If you are suffering from anxiety or depression or both, your learning is probably going to be compromised. This is the reality of our schools at present.

What is the purpose of education from a Catholic perspective? In 1977, the Prefect for the Vatican Congregation for Catholic Education at the time, Cardinal Garrone, published a seminal document called *The Catholic School*. One of the often-quoted lines from the document states that the purpose of Catholic Education is

> …*a synthesis of culture and faith, and a synthesis of faith and life: the first is reached by integrating all the different aspects of human knowledge through the subjects taught, in the light of the Gospel; the second in the growth of the virtues characteristic of the Christian.*[7]

Education in a Catholic setting cannot be static, it needs to respond to the changing culture, read the 'signs of the times,'[8] and respond in light of the Gospel. Cardinal Garrone's instruction to synthesise faith, culture and life is not only wise, it is also practical. Given that culture is never static, I think it is worth taking a little time to look at the world we live in and how we have got there. To understand

---

[5] J. Perera, et al, *Presentations to NSW emergency departments with self-harm, suicidal ideation, or intentional poisoning, 2010–2014*, 2018, Box 3.
[6] Mission Australia, *Youth Mental Health Report*, 2017.
[7] G. Garrone, *The Catholic School*, 1977, Section 37.
[8] Paul VI, 1965, *Gravissimum Educationis. Declaration on Christian Education*, Section 4.

ourselves, we have to understand history and the ideas that have shaped us.

Up until the Middle Ages and Early Modern period (up until perhaps 1789), a large proportion of the Western world was Christian. There was an attendant surety of meaning and metaphysical order provided by the Church, which permeated all aspects of life. The dominance of the Catholic Church and Christian metaphysics was challenged by the Reformation, the Scientific Revolution, the Enlightenment and the rise in secularism and atheism. The search for meaning also became more secular, focused on this world and individualised. The responsibility for finding meaning slowly transferred from being a societal given to an individual concern. The collective adherence to the assumed dogmatic metaphysical order was slowly eroded and replaced by individual subjective experience. Wardle argued that the individual enquiry as to the meaning of life arises in the nineteenth century.[9]

Going back to the sixteenth century, Copernicus initiated a new way of thinking and understanding of cosmology that moved planet earth and the human beings on it from being at the centre of the universe. Instead, the human being was now one more creature on one more planet which exists among billions of other planets in an indifferent universe. The human subject's conception of his place and significance in the cosmos shifted from being at the centre and pinnacle of creation to one of demotion to comparative insignificance. The revolutions in Science spilled over into philosophy. Philosophers such as Descartes and Kant, though devoutly Christian themselves, showed that human knowledge was a lot less certain than previously understood. Kant believed that God, the transcendent and metaphysics generally are not matters of knowledge but matters of faith.

---

[9] D. Wardle *The Meaning(s) of Life: A Contemporary Perspective Between Nietzsche, Sartre & Nancy*, 2016, p. 10.

Kant maintained a belief in a transcendent world, the noumenon, which for Kant was not part of the phenomenal world. Kant's insights removed some of the previously existing metaphysical certainty.

Karl Marx argued that religion was a fantasy world designed to make people feel better as they are unhappy, oppressed and alienated due to their working lives. Nietzsche took Kant's distinction between phenomenal and noumenal knowledge a step further and advocated for the end of God, religion, idealism and metaphysics. Nietzsche's pronouncement of the death of God compromised foundational conceptions of truth and meaning that had been held as the metaphysical order for centuries. The notion of the death of God was in effect a challenge to the notion of objective truth. Nietzsche also advocated perspectivism – there are different points of view and perspectives, which leads to relativism. Which in turn leads to nihilism and pessimism as there is no hierarchy of values and meaning.

Sartre took Nietzsche's ideas about the loss of objective truth and advocated that an individual's existence precedes societal structures and norms and expectations. The individual is free of psychological predispositions and societal expectations. Sartre's existentialism propounded that the human subject is alone in the world. Following on from Nietzsche, Sartre agrees that there is no ground for morals or values. The individual is free to create their own morality. Sartre argues that nihilism and its attendant freedom to create one's own life is to be celebrated. However, for many, this radical freedom and the responsibility that goes with it is a source of fear and even anguish.

Part of the human condition seems to be the need to makes sense of oneself and the world we live in. The revolutions in thought I've mentioned removed some of the long held foundational beliefs that were taken for granted for millennia. Armstrong writes 'we are meaning seeking creatures...human beings fall easily into despair, and from the very beginning we invented stories that enabled us to place our lives in a larger setting, that revealed an underlying pattern, and gave us a sense that, against all the depressing and chaotic evidence to the contrary, life had meaning and value.'[10] The revolutions of thought described have undermined and eroded these structures and narratives. One of the main causes of the loss of meaning is postmodernism. Postmodernism was defined by Lyotard as 'incredulity towards metanarratives.'[11] That is, 'where metanarratives are understood as totalising stories about history and the goals of the human race that ground and legitimise knowledges and cultural practises.'[12] The human subject seeks meaning in a universe which cannot be understood but only be interpreted in its essence. The individual seeks meaning in a universe that is meaningless and impersonal according to many nineteenth and twentieth century thinkers such as Marx, Nietzsche and Sartre.

Moving to the twentieth century, Freud advocated that many of the drives of being human are subconscious or unconscious. This was another blow to the human subject's liberty and freedom. Not only is planet Earth not the centre of the universe and the human subject just one more species on that planet, but the human subject was not even in control of its own choices and drives. Turner argued that Freud democratised the search for happiness 'through popular therapies such as yoga, self-help strategies and by the adoption of psychedelic and recreational drugs such as cannabis and Prozac that, if they do not deliver lasting happiness, offered relief from the cycle of depression.'[13]

---

[10] K. Armstrong 2005, p. 2.
[11] J. Lyotard, cited in A. Woodward, *Internet Encyclopedia of Philosophy*, para. 18.
[12] Ibid.
[13] B. S. Turner, cited in: Y. Contreras-Vejar, J. Tice Jen, B. S. and Turner, *Regimes of Happiness: Comparative and Historical Studies*, 2019, p. 28.

Turner goes on to note that there were many self-actualisation movements in the 1960s that included aspects of Eastern religions and experimentation with drugs and sex.

While I have painted a fairly bleak picture in describing these new understandings of cosmology and human beings' place within it, for the sake of balance, I'll mention Steven Pinker, author of *The Better Angels of our Nature* (2011) and *Enlightenment Now* (2018). I don't have time to discuss Pinker's views in detail, he does have a much more optimistic view of the modern world, human progress and the improvements in the quality of life.

Teenagers of today are the heirs, and it might be said victims of these movements and the way they have formed the world we live in today. Although the average teenager is probably oblivious to these historical movements, they have been thrust into a world where the norms and advice on how to live have evolved from the major currents of thought that have preceded them. Wardle describes the situation as 'a personal problematic for individuals who had become increasingly atomized, socially isolated, and abandoned to a world without epistemic or metaphysical certitude, leaving individuals without a secure foundation for their personal meaning in life.'[14] I think this picture is part of the reason for the magnitude of the anxiety and depression teenagers are now experiencing.

We know that the internet and social media are relatively recent phenomena that are an integral part of the lives of most teenagers. Taylor notes that two deep human needs are close, intimate relationships and solitude. Taylor goes on to state that social media achieve neither. A person on social media is neither alone nor in face-to-face company with another human being. More face-to-face socialising produces oxytocin, which increases productivity, reduces self-interest, increases psychological safety, altruism and

---

[14] D. Wardle, *The Meaning(s) of Life: A Contemporary Perspective Between Nietzsche, Sartre & Nancy*. 2016, p. 11.

teamwork. Social media for many is an attempt to fill a loneliness gap. Face to face connection is far more effective. Over the past 40-50 years, social networks have become dismantled due to the rise in individualism which has contributed to the loneliness of many. We know that membership of trade unions, churches, political parties and so forth has reduced significantly.

So far I have given you some data on the life of teenagers and some of the movements that have brought us to the world we now live in. I now want to give an alternative narrative which proposes some solutions to improving teenager wellbeing and the possibility of openness to a faith life. This narrative emphasises meaning, purpose, service, encounter, love and liberation. I argue that students can experience this through theological formation, service education opportunities and prayer and reflection. Metaphorically, this is the head, heart and hands approach I mentioned earlier.

We all need meaning and purpose, which is an antidote to anxiety and depression. Viktor Frankl wrote one of the most iconic books of the Twentieth Century, *Man's Search for Meaning*. As we know, Frankl and most of his family were sent to the Nazi death camps. Most of his family perished in the camps. Frankl's main work as a psychologist after the war was the development of logotherapy. Faramarzi and Bavali, (2017) state that logotherapy's main contention is that 'lack of meaning is the chief source of stress as well as anxiety, and logotherapy aids the patients to reach the meaning of life'.[15] Frankl in the extremes of the Nazi death camps saw that some were able to find meaning in these inhuman conditions. They were the ones who were the more resilient to the immense suffering they endured.

Thomas Nielsen, an academic from Canberra agrees with Frankl, and many others in believing that meaning increases wellbeing. Nielsen argues that deeper and longer lasting

---

[15] Faramarzi and Bavali, cited in J. Selva, Logotherapy: Viktor Frankl's Theory of Meaning. *PositivePsychology.com*. 2017, para. 3.

happiness and meaning come from serving others. Nielsen argues that there is one common denominator of meaning regardless of culture, race and religion and that is '… "being something" to someone or something other than themselves'[16] One of the outcomes of this way of life according to a number of theorists is transcendence – of space, time and oneself, which is liberating.

This transcendence of self often takes place through encounter with the other. Buber and Levinas have written beautifully on how encounter with the other can be transformative for both parties. The Christian Brother Damien Price after a lifetime of working with young people in service contexts has a similar view: 'the most profound conversion experience for the young people I have taken down there has come about because of the entry into the sacred space of someone's story.'[17] It is in the encounter with another person that transformation for both parties is possible. Elizabeth Dunn has noted that we have evolved to find joy in helping others. Dunn states: 'we need to create opportunities to give that enable us that enable us to appreciate our shared humanity.'[18] From Dunn's perspective, giving then becomes a source of pleasure rather than a moral obligation. Br Michael Flanagan, former Vocations promoter for the Marist Brothers in an article in April this year wrote: 'all human beings have the same Vocation: we are born to be human for others.'[19]

---

[16] T. Nielsen, Finding the Keys to Meaningful Happiness: Beyond Being Happy or Sad is to Love. *Meaning in Positive and Existential Psychology*. 2014, p. 84.

[17] D. Price, *The Road Less travelled: the theological journey of young people*, n.d., p. 6

[18] E. Dunn, Elizabeth Dunn: Helping others makes us happier - but it matters how we do it [Video file], *TED Talk*, 2019.

[19] M. Flanagan, 2021, A Reflection of Vocation, *Christlife Newsletter*, Vol 103, para. 3.

Buber, Frankl and Levinas were all great Jewish thinkers. Christianity in my reading is more explicit in its focus on charity or love as the supreme value. Yiu and Vorster stated 'in the order of perfection, Aquinas puts charity (love) before faith and hope in that: ... both faith and hope are formed by charity and so acquire the perfection of virtue. Charity is thus the mother and root of all virtues insofar as it is the form of all virtues.'[20]

Pope Benedict stated in his first encyclical, *Deus Caritas Est*: 'Love is therefore the service that the Church carries out in order to attend constantly to man's sufferings and his needs, including material needs.'[21] And again from Pope Benedict: 'practical activity will always be insufficient, unless it visibly expresses a love for man, a love nourished by an encounter with Christ. ... I must give to others not only something that is my own, but my very self; I must be personally present in my gift.'[22]

For John Paul II, the phrase 'self-giving' was a key motif of his papacy. Voxnovablog notes that the phrase 'man can fully discover his true self only in a sincere giving of himself'[23] has metaphysical, anthropological, moral and social implications. The statement is also paradoxical. As Voxnovablog puts it, 'how utterly curious that I am a self that, in its very selfhood, loses itself but in so doing fully finds and recovers itself.'[24] The liberation and wellbeing described earlier with transcendence of self, space and time in Christian terms may be described as *kenosis,* or self-emptying. Oord (2015, p. 219) describes *kenosis* as 'self-

---

[20] S. Yiu & J. M. Vorster, 'The goal of Christian virtue ethics: From ontological foundation and covenant relationship to the Kingdom of God', cited in *die Skriflig/ In Luce Verbi* 47(1), 1971.
[21] Benedict XVI, *Deus Caritas Est.*, 2005, Section 19.
[22] Ibid, Section 34.
[23] Gaudium et spes, section 24, cited in Voxnovablog, *Karol Wojtyła (John Paul II) on Self-Giving.* 2007, para. 1.
[24] Voxnovablog, *Karol Wojtyła (John Paul II) on Self-Giving.* 2007, para. 13.

giving, others empowering love'.²⁵ In Christianity, similar to Judaism, the transcendence achieved by encounter and service leads one to encounter with the sacred, with God.

Pope Francis in his recent Encyclical *Fratelli Tutti* states:

> *At a time when everything seems to disintegrate and lose consistency, it is good for us to appeal to the "solidity" born of the consciousness that we are responsible for the fragility of others as we strive to build a common future. Solidarity finds concrete expression in service, which can take a variety of forms in an effort to care for others. And service in great part means "caring for vulnerability, for the vulnerable members of our families, our society, our people". In offering such service, individuals learn to "set aside their own wishes and desires, their pursuit of power, before the concrete gaze of those who are most vulnerable... Service always looks to their faces, touches their flesh, senses their closeness and even, in some cases, 'suffers' that closeness and tries to help them. Service is never ideological, for we do not serve ideas, we serve people.*²⁶

The Australian Aboriginal Lilla Watson is attributed with saying 'if you have come here to help me, you are wasting your time. But if you have come because your liberation is bound up with mine, then let us work together.'²⁷

As I have now discussed, a number of writers believe that loving service can create meaning and purpose. The giving of oneself can lead to the possibility of transcending time, space and oneself. This is both liberating and revealing in that one learns about oneself. The ancient Greek word for truth was *aletheia*, which means that truth is revealed or disclosed. The giving of oneself paradoxically helps in the process of self- discovery and growing into one's best self.

---

²⁵ T. J. Oord, *The Uncontrolling Love of God: An Open and Relational Account of Providence.* 2005, p. 219.
²⁶ Francis, *Fratelli Tutti*, n. 115.
²⁷ L. Watson, cited by S. Thomson, *My Liberation is Bound Up With Yours.* 2016, para. 6.

Where are we up to? After giving an account of the slide of the modern world into individualism and a lack of meaning, I have given an alternative narrative of the importance of meaning, purpose, encounter, love, transcendence, and liberation. How can these lofty aspirations be achieved for our teenagers? What does this look like in terms of the spiritual and faith formation of teenagers.

A mix of theological formation, service learning and reflection helps with the faith life and wellbeing of teenagers. This is the formation of head, hearts and hands. In my experience of teaching more than 40 Religious Education classes, in my roles as Religious Education Coordinator, Director of Ministry and Principal, I have found that it is the most effective means of formation. Education of the head is about age-appropriate theological formation. Formation of the heart is prayer and reflection opportunities. Formation of the hands is experiential education through service experiences to others. This where the encounter usually takes place which is so transformative. Programs with a mix of these three areas are effective, life giving for students and sometimes, even occasionally life changing for students, a bold claim, I know. One example from personal experience not all that long ago was offering a subject called Theology and Ministry as an elective, which was a mix of head, heart, and hands as I described. It went from 10 students to 38 students in one year. To be clear, these are Year 9 students choosing to do a second class of Religious Education, as an elective. Not only was it effective, but it was also popular. Students wanted to do it. It was also some of the most effective faith development I have seen, far more so than the average Religious Education class.

Why is this approach to education not only effective, but also sometimes transformative?

There is a lot of literature by people such as Mezirow, Dewey, Kolb, Deren, Bridges and Price who describe and explain the psychological processes taking place in service learning. Very briefly, life provides what Mezirow (1991) calls disorienting dilemmas which challenge one's existing beliefs about reality. In my last two schools we had students take part in immersions to Timor Leste, which is a strong example of a disorienting dilemma with the students' existing mental frames of reference being confronted with new perspectives. Learning takes place when we are able to revise our interpretation of an experience even though there is often some discomfort in doing so. A new worldview can emerge. Kolb writes that the 'the normal flow of experience must be interrupted by deep experiencing, such as when we are 'stuck' with a problem or difficulty or "struck" by the strangeness of something outside of our usual experience.'[28] It is these experiences which evoke new insights and changes in behaviour and perhaps an openness to faith. Service learning provides opportunities for the encounters which can be transformative.

Students have reported to me many times over the years that a mix of theological formation, outreach and reflection has been transformative for them. I recall the first morning of a new term a few years ago where I asked a young man how his immersion to Timor went. He said he was very moved and in fact wanted to join a religious order. This was a student of no religious affiliation. No doubt he was caught up in the emotion of the experience. That is why the foundations of formation of the mind is so important, as emotions come and go. Religious Education gives a language to help understand these experiences.

Faith is not passed on by families for the most part these days. Our Catholic schools are one of the main sources which have the capacity to pass on the faith. This is always by invitation, as Jesus always invited. We need to have faith filled staff who pass on the richness of our tradition, accompany students and provide prayer and reflection opportunities, which may open the door to the living Christ.

---

[28] A. & D. Kolb, *Experiential Learning as a Guide for Educators*, 2018, p. 24.

We need to have faith that the rest is between each individual and their God. My experience has been that improved wellbeing and the possibility of openness to faith is more likely to occur through an emphasis on relationships and a mix of theological formation, service activities and prayer and reflection.

Bibliography

Australian Institute of Health and Welfare, The (2021) *The use of mental health services, psychological distress, loneliness, suicide, ambulance attendances and COVID-19.* Accessed: 11/7/21. Retrieved from: https://www.aihw.gov.au/suicide-self-harm-monitoring/data/covid-19

Armstrong, K. (2005) *A Short History of Myth.* Melbourne: The Text Publishing Company

Astin, A.W., Vogelgesang, L. J., Ikeda, E. K., and Yee, J. E. (2000) How Service Learning Affects Students. *Higher Education Research Institute University of California*, Los Angeles. Accessed 9/1/19. Retrieved from: https://www.heri.ucla.edu/PDFs/HSLAS/HSLAS.PDF

Australian Bureau of Statistics (2018) *National Health Survey: First results.* Accessed: 28/12/20. Retrieved from: https://www.abs.gov.au/statistics/health/health-conditions-and-risks/national-health-survey-first-results/latest-release

Bachelard, S. (2016, April), *A Spirituality of Service Learning.* Paper presented at the biannual conference: Transformational Service. An ecumenical conference for educators and leaders in service leaders. Melbourne, Victoria, Australia.

Bandy, J. (n.d.) *What is Service Learning or Community Engagement?* Accessed 23/8/19. Retrieved from: https://cft.vanderbilt.edu/guides-sub-pages/teaching-through-community-engagement/

Baumeistera R.F., Vohs K.D, Aakerc, J.L. and Garbinsky, E.N. (2013) Some key differences between a happy life and a meaningful life. *The Journal of Positive Psychology.* Accessed: 10/2/19. Retrieved from: http://eds.b.ebscohost.com.ezproxy.utas.edu.au/eds/pdfviewer/pdfviewer?vid=1&sid=123d6ba9-b228-47fb-a15a-f5c341f09cc9%40sessionmgr120

Becker, P.A. (2013) The Contribution of Emmanuel Levinas to Corporate Social Responsibility and Business Ethics in the Post-Modern Era. *Journal of International Business Ethics.* Accessed 11/2/19. Retrieved from: http://eds.a.ebscohost.com.ezproxy.utas.edu.au

Bergo, B. (2017) Emmanuel Levinas. *The Stanford Encyclopedia of Philosophy* Accessed 2/2/19. Retrieved from: https://plato.stanford.edu/archives/fall2017/entries/levinas/

Beyond Blue (n.d.) *Building Resilience in Children.* Accessed from: 6/4/19. Retrieved from: https://healthyfamilies.beyondblue.org.au/healthy-homes/building-resilience

Bisson, R. & Stubley, W. (2017). After the ATAR: Understanding How Gen Z Transition into Further Education and Employment *Year13*, Australia.

Black Dog Institute. *Depression in adolescents & young people.* Accessed 14/5/18. Retrieved from: https://www.blackdoginstitute.org.au/docs/default-source/factsheets/depressioninadolescents.pdf?sfvrsn=2

Buber, M. (1937) *I and Thou.* London: Reprint Continuum International Publishing Group, 2004

Canales, A. D. (2009) A noble quest: cultivating Christian spirituality in Catholic adolescents and the usefulness of 12 pastoral practices. *International Journal of Children's Spirituality Vol. 14.* Accessed 19/3/19. Retrieved from: https://www.tandfonline.com/doi/full/10.1080/13644360802658768

Carlisle, E., Fildes, J., Hall, S., Hicking, V., Perrens, B., & Plummer, J. (2018). *Youth Survey Report 2018*. Mission Australia.

Cluey Learning (2020) *Research series p3: How Covid-19 has affected stress and study*. Accessed: 11/7/21. Retrieved from: https://clueylearning.com.au/blog/how-covid-19-has-affected-stress-and-study/

Contreras-Vejar, Y., Tice Jen, J. and Turner. B. S. (2019) *Regimes of Happiness: Comparative and Historical Studies*, London: Anthem Press.

Deren, J. (n.d.) *Transformative Education and Catholic Social Teaching*. Accessed: 11/3/18. Retrieved from: http://www.erea.edu.au/docs/default-source/justice-peace/tranformative-education-jane-deren.pdf?sfvrsn=368a7f68_2

Dewey, J. (1910) *How we think*. Boston, MA: D.C. Heath.

Dewey, J. (2011) *Democracy and Education*. Milton Keynes: Simon and Brown

Dunn, E (2019, April) *Elizabeth Dunn: Helping others makes us happier - but it matters how we do it* [Video file]. Accessed: 28/4/19. Retrieved from: https://www.ted.com/talks/elizabeth_dunn_helping_others_makes_us_happier_but_it_matters_how_we_do_it?language=en

Earp, J. (2017) Mental health biggest issue for youth. Teacher bulletin. *Australian Council for Educational Research*. Accessed 4/1/21. Retrieved from: https://www.teachermagazine.com/au_en/articles/mental-health-biggest-issue-for-youth

Edmund Rice Education Beyond Borders (2017) Edmund Rice Education and Values. *Leadership Certificate, Module 2*. Accessed 15/1/18. Retrieved from: https://mie.learnonline.ie/course/view.php?id=865

Eyler, J. and Giles, D.E. (1999) *Where's the Learning in Service-Learning?* San Francisco: Jossey-Bass Publishers.

Francis (2020) *Fratelli Tutti. On Fraternity and Social Friendship*. Accessed: 27/6/21. Retrieved from:

https://www.vatican.va/content/francesco/en/encyclicals/documents/papa-francesco_20201003_enciclica-fratelli-tutti.html

Frankl, V. E. (1985) *Man's Search for Meaning: An Introduction to Logotherapy.* New York: Pocket Books.

Furco, A. (1996) "Service-Learning: A Balanced Approach to Experiential Education." *Expanding Boundaries: Service and Learning.* Washington DC: Corporation for National Service. Accessed 9/1/19. Retrieved from: http://www.wou.edu/~girodm/670/service_learning.pdf

Garrone, G. (1977) *The Catholic School.* The Sacred Congregation for Catholic Education. Accessed: 4/1/19. Retrieved from: http://www.vatican.va/roman_curia/congregations/ccatheduc/documents/rc_con_ccatheduc_doc_19770319_catholic-school_en.html

Green, P. M. (2006). *Service-reflection-learning: An action research study of the meaning-making processes occurring through reflection in a Service Learning course.* Unpublished Ed D thesis in the Department of Educational Leadership and Organizational Change. Chicago: Roosevelt University.

Grohol, J. and Telloian, C. (2021) *Depression Causes and Risk Factors.* Psych Central. Accessed: 3/4/21. Retrieved from: https://psychcentral.com/depression/depression-causes

Hall, G. (n.d.) *Human Rights Education: Transformative Learning Through Student Participation in Extracurricular Activities at School.*

Haybron, D. M. (2014) Happiness and Its Discontents *The New York Times.* Accessed 2/1/19. Retrieved from: https://opinionator.blogs.nytimes.com/author/daniel-m-haybron/

Headspace (2018) *New headspace research reveals alarming levels of psychological distress in young Australians.* Accessed 18/3/19. Retrieved from: https://headspace.org.au/blog/new-headspace-research-reveals-alarming-levels-of-psychological-distress-in-young-australians/

Headspace (2020) *Coping with COVID: the mental health impact on young people accessing headspace services August 2020.* Accessed: 11/7/21. Retrieved from: https://headspace.org.au/assets/Uploads/COVID-Client-Impact-Report-FINAL-11-8-20.pdf

Holland, J. and Henriot, P. (1983) *Social Analysis: Lining Faith and Justice* Maryknoll, NY: Orbis and Washington, DC

Joshanloo, M., & Jarden, A. (2016). Individualism as the moderator of the relationship between hedonism and happiness: A study in 19 nations. *Personality and Individual Differences, 94*, 149-152. Accessed 14/6/21. Retrieved from: http://www.aaronjarden.com/uploads/3/8/0/4/3804146/individualism_as_the_moderator_of_the_relationship_between_hedonism_and_happiness_draft.pdf

Kenny, A. (2012) *A New History of Western Philosophy.* Oxford: Clarendon Press.

Kolb, A&D. (Term 2, 2018) *Australian Educational Leader* (Magazine). Vol 40, Issue 2.

Kolb, D. (2018, October) *Experiential Learning as a Guide for Educators.* Paper presented at the Australian Council for Educational Leaders National Conference, Melbourne.

Lambert, H. and Robbins, L. (2018) *Grassroot Stories: Growing Concepts, Changing Culture.* Paper presented at the biannual Transforming Service Conference. Accessed 20/4/19. Retrieved from: http://www.transformingservice.com/uploads/1/1/9/3/11936953/grassroots_stories_helenalambert_laurarobbins_final.pdf

Law, S. (2007) *The Great Philosophers.* London: Quercus.

Lenoir, F. (2013) *Happiness. A Philosopher's Guide.* Brooklyn, NY: Melville House Publishing.

Levinas, E. (1989) Is Ontology Fundamental? *Philosophy Today.* Accessed: 9/2/19. Retrieved from: https://www.pdcnet.org/philtoday/content/philtoday_1989_0033_0002_0121_0129

Loughnane, M. (2008) *Fashioning a Dialogical Vision for Catholic Education through Analysis, Critique and Contemporisation of Paulo Freire's Education as the Practice of Freedom.* A thesis submitted in fulfilment of the requirements for the degree of Doctor of Philosophy to the Melbourne College of Divinity.

Løvoll, H.S. (2019) The inner feeling of glacier hiking: an exploratory study of "immersion" as it relates to flow, hedonia and eudaimonia, *Scandinavian Journal of Hospitality and Tourism*, 19:3, 300-316, DOI: 10.1080/15022250.2019.1581084 Accessed 13/7/20. Retrieved from: https://www-tandfonline-com.ezproxy.utas.edu.au/doi/full/10.1080/15022250.2019.1581084

McGreal, I. (1992) *Great Thinkers of the Western World.* New York: Collins Reference

McMahon, D.M. (2004) From the happiness of virtue to the virtue of happiness: 400B.C. – A.D. 1780. *Daedalus.* Spring, 2004, Vol. 133 Issue 2. Retrieved from: https://www.jstor.org/stable/20027908?seq=3#metadata_info_tab_contents Accessed: 11/11/20.

McMahon, D. M. (2006) *Happiness: A History.* Atlantic Monthly Press. Retrieved from: Accessed: 10/11/20

Mezirow, J. (1991) *Transformative dimensions of adult education.* San Francisco: Jossey-Bass Inc.

Mission Australia (2017) *Youth Mental Health Report.* Accessed 2/4/19. Retrieved from: https://blackdoginstitute.org.au/docs/default-source/research/evidence-and-policy-section/2017-youth-mental-health-report_mission-australia-and-black-dog-institute.pdf?sfvrsn=6

Mojtabai, R., Olfson, M., Han, B. *National Trends in the Prevalence and Treatment of Depression in Adolescents and Young Adults.* Accessed 17/6/18. Retrieved from: http://pediatrics.aappublications.org/content/early/2016/11/10/peds.2016-1878

Nelson, J. & Slife, B. (2017) A new positive psychology: A critique of the movement based on early Christian thought. *The Journal of Positive Psychology.* Accessed: 13/2/19. Retrieved from: https://www-tandfonline-com.ezproxy.utas.edu.au/doi/pdf/10.1080/17439760.2016.1228006

New World Encyclopedia contributors. (2017) Emmanuel Lévinas. *New World Encyclopedia.* Accessed 2/2/19. Retrieved from http://www.newworldencyclopedia.org/p/index.php?title=Emmanuel_L%C3%A9vinas&oldid=1006647.

Nielsen, T.W. (2014) Finding the Keys to Meaningful Happiness: Beyond Being Happy or Sad is to Love. *Meaning in Positive and Existential Psychology.* Accessed 27/1/19. Retrieved from: https://www.researchgate.net/publication/294286097_Finding_the_Keys_to_Meaningful_Happiness_Beyond_Being_Happy_or_Sad_is_to_Love

Neilsen, T. W. (2015) Happy? Consider how giving builds a life of meaning. *Curriculum of Giving.* Accessed 19/1/19. Retrieved from: http://www.thomaswnielsen.net/happy-consider-how-giving-builds-a-life-of-meaning/

Odriozola, P. & Gee, D. (2018) Developing teen brains are vulnerable to anxiety – but treatment can help. *The Conversation.* Accessed 7/6/21. Retrieved from: Oord, T. J. (2015) *The Uncontrolling Love of God: An Open and Relational Account of Providence.* Illinois: Inter Varsity Press.

Paul VI. (1965a) *Gravissimum Educationis Declaration on Christian education.* Accessed 29.6.18. Retrieved from: http://www.vatican.va/archive/hist_councils/ii_vatican_council/documents/vat-ii_decl_19651028_gravissimum-educationis_en.html

Paul VI. (1965b). *Pastoral Constitution on the Church in the modern world: Gaudium et spes.* Accessed: 4/9/19. Retrieved from: http://www.vatican.va/archive/hist_councils/ii_vatican_c

ouncil/documents/vat-ii_const_19651207_gaudium-et-spes_en.html

Perera, J., Bein, K.J., Chalkley, D., Ivers, R., Steinbeck, K.S., Shields, R., Dinh, M.M., (2018) *Presentations to NSW emergency departments with self-harm, suicidal ideation, or intentional poisoning, 2010–2014*. Education Review, Issue 4 June 2018.

Peters, R. S. (1963). Education as initiation. Inaugural lecture delivered at the Institute of Education, University of London, London, 9 December.

Pinker, S. (2014) *The Village Effect*. London; Atlantic Books.

Premier Health (2017) *Beware High Levels of Cortisol, the Stress Hormone*. Accessed 30/9/2020. Retrieved from: https://www.premierhealth.com/your-health/articles/women-wisdom-wellness-/beware-high-levels-of-cortisol-the-stress-hormone#:~:text=As%20your%20body%20perceives%20stress,alive%20for%20thousands%20of%20years.

Price, D. (2012, July) *The processes involved in Service Learning*. Professional Article prepared for the EREA Service and Solidarity Conference – Richmond, Melbourne, Victoria, Australia.

Price. D. (2016, April) *Transformation or Ticking Boxes; taking Service Learning Seriously*. Paper presented at the biannual conference: Transformational Service. An ecumenical conference for educators and leaders in service leaders. Melbourne, Victoria, Australia.

Price, D. (n.d.) *The Road Less travelled: the theological journey of young people*. No publisher details.

Pullen, D. *Personal Communication*, 2/3/18.

Rabbas, O., Emilsson, E. K., Fosshweim, H., and Tuominen, M. (2015) *The Quest for the Good Life*. Oxford: Oxford University Press.

Rodriguez, D. (2020) *How to Cope With Anxiety and Depression*. Accessed: 4/421. Retrieved from: https://www.everydayhealth.com/anxiety/anxiety-and-depression.aspx

Roebben, B. (2012) *Kenosis, Human Flourishing and Solidarity: Re-Thinking the Goal of Education in Late-Modernity.* Accessed 22/1/19. Retrieved from: https://religiouseducation.net/rea2012/files/2012/10/RIG3.5-Roebben.pdf

Rockliff, J. Minister for Education and Training, 11 October 2017 *Vale Professor Eleanor Ramsay.* Accessed 27.5.18. Retrieved from Media Release http://www.premier.tas.gov.au/releases/vale_professor_eleanor_ramsay

Root, E, Ngampornchai, A. (2012) 'I Came Back as a New Human Being': Student Descriptions of Intercultural Competence Acquired Through Education Abroad. *Journal of Studies in International Education* 17(5) 513–532 © 2012. Accessed 22/8/20. Retrieved from: https://journals-sagepub-com.ezproxy.utas.edu.au/doi/pdf/10.1177/1028315312468008

Royal Society for Public Health (2015) *#StatusofMind.* Accessed 23/5/18. Retrieved from: https://www.rsph.org.uk/our-work/campaigns/status-of-mind.html

Salcedo, B. (2018) *The Comorbidity of Anxiety and Depression.* Accessed: 4/4/21. Retrieved from: https://www.nami.org/Blogs/NAMI-Blog/January-2018/The-Comorbidity-of-Anxiety-and-Depression

Schacter, H. L., & Margolin, G. (2019). When it feels good to give: Depressive symptoms, daily prosocial behavior, and adolescent mood. *Emotion, 19*(5), 923–927. Accessed 4/10/20. Retrieved from: http://ovidsp.dc2.ovid.com.ezproxy.utas.edu.au/ovida/ovidweb.cgi?

_Selva, J. (2017) Logotherapy: Viktor Frankl's Theory of Meaning. *PositivePsychology.com.* Accessed: 12/4/19. Retrieved from: https://positivepsychology.com/viktor-frankl-logotherapy/

Shelton, C.M. (1983) *Adolescent Spirituality. Pastoral Ministry for High School and College Youth.* New York: The Crossroad Publishing Company.

Sigmon, R. (1979) quoted in Furco, Andrew. "Service-Learning: A Balanced Approach to Experiential Education." *Expanding Boundaries: Service and Learning.* Washington DC: Corporation for National Service, 1996. 2-6.

Smith, C. (2016) *A Liberating Education.* Accessed 30.5.18. Retrieved from personal communication.

Smith, E. (2013) Meaning comes from the pursuit of more complex things than happiness *The Atlantic.* Accessed 10/1/19. Retrieved from: https://www.theatlantic.com/health/archive/2013/01/theres-more-to-life-than-being-happy/266805/

Smith, E. (2017) *The Power of Meaning.* London: Penguin Random House.

Smith, E. (2021) "Teen Anguish in the Pandemic." *New York Times, Gale Academic OneFile.* Retrieved from: link.gale.com/apps/doc/A661174608/AONE?u=utas1&sid=AONE&xid=bd4bc74f. Accessed 26 May 2021.

Symonds, M. (1995) *Social and Political Philosophy 1: The Western Tradition.* Lecture notes. University of Western Sydney, Nepean.

Tarnas, R. (1989) The transfiguration of the Western Mind. *Cross Currents.* Accessed: 9/4/21. Retrieved from: https://www-jstor-org.ezproxy.utas.edu.au/stable/pdf/24459175.pdf?refreqid=excelsior%3A793ac74e01ea0f578066a2c2f81dc99c

Tarnas, R. (1993) *The Passion of the Western Mind.* New York: Ballantine Books.

Taylor, D. (2019) *Loneliness and the Search for the Self.* The Henry Baldwin Lecture. St George's, Battery Point.

Thomson, P. (2010) *Whole school change: a literature review.* Creativity, Culture and education Review Series. Newcastle upon Tyne: Arts Council England.

Thomson, S. (2016) *My Liberation is Bound Up With Yours*. Accessed 19/9/19. Retrieved from: https://www.alifeoverseas.com/my-liberation-is-bound-up-with-yours/

_Tinsey, W. (2014) *Touchstones: Stories, Thoughts and Reflections on Catholic Education and the Christian Vision*. Kew East, Victoria: David Lovell Publishing.

Tomyn, A. (2014) *Youth Connections Subjective Wellbeing Report*. Accessed 19/5/18. Retrieved from: https://docs.education.gov.au/documents/subjective-wellbeing-young-people-youth-connections

Tomyn, A., Weinberg, M.K., (2016) *Resilience and Subjective Wellbeing: A Psychometric Evaluation in Young Australian Adults*. Accessed 28.4.18. Retrieved from: https://onlinelibrary-wiley-com.ezproxy.utas.edu.au/doi/full/10.1111/ap.12251

Uchida, Y., Norasakkunkit, V. & Kitayama, S. (2004) Cultural constructions of happiness: theory and empirical evidence. *Journal of Happiness Studies* **5,** 223–239. Accessed 16/6/21. Retrieved from:
https://doi.org/10.1007/s10902-004-8785-9

Vogel, L. A. (2008) *Emmanuel Levinas and the Judaism of the Good Samaritan*. Accessed 11/2/19. Retrieved from:
https://digitalcommons.conncoll.edu/cgi/viewcontent.cgi?referer=https://www.google.com/&httpsredir=1&article=1004&context=philfacpub

Voxnovablog. (2007) *Karol Wojtyła (John Paul II) on Self-Giving*. Accessed 24/1/19. Retrieved from: https://www.patheos.com/blogs/voxnova/2007/05/23/karol-wojtyla-john-paul-ii-on-self-giving/

Vukovic, D. (2017) *One in three higher education students think about suicide or self-harm, report says*. Accessed on 16/4/18. Retrieved from: http://www.abc.net.au/news/2017-04-06/one-in-three-students-consider-self-harm-and-suicide/8420728

_Vukovic, R. (2021) The impact of loneliness. *Wellbeing by Teacher*. Accessed 30/4/21. Retrieved from:
https://www.teachermagazine.com/au_en/articles/the-

impact-of-loneliness?utm_source=CM&utm_medium=Wellbeing&utm_term=24April

Ward, D. (2016) *The Meaning(s) of Life: A Contemporary Perspective Between Nietzsche, Sartre & Nancy.* Accessed: 4/6/21. Retrieved from: https://repository.up.ac.za/bitstream/handle/2263/60441/Wardle_Meaning_2016.pdf?sequence=1&isAllowed=y

What is a Good Life? (2013, February 13) *The Week.* Accessed 9/2/19. Retrieved from: https://theweek.com/articles/467658/what-good-life

_Woodward, A. (n.d.) Jean-Francois Lyotard (1924 – 1998) Internet Encyclopedia of Philosophy. Accessed: 14/4/21. Retrieved from: https://iep.utm.edu/lyotard/

A CHRISTIAN ANTHROPOLOGICAL CREED

Archbishop Julian Porteous

Christians are very familiar with the idea of a creed which encapsulates the essential elements of our belief. At Mass every Sunday we say the Nicaean Creed. We recite the Apostles Creed when we say the Rosary. As we say the words of the creed we punctuate the statements with 'I believe', *Credo* in Latin. A creed is a formularised confession of the Christian faith. The Creed distils the faith in summary form. They have proved helpful touchstones for orthodoxy.

Changes in understanding the Human Person

Social changes are sweeping our culture and significantly altering the way people view the nature of the human person especially in the areas of the understanding of marriage, of gender, of sexuality. It is true that now the bulk of Australians have an understanding of human nature which conflicts with the Christian understanding, which itself has guided Western civilisation for around the last 1500 years. This Christian understanding is being systematically challenged and removed as the guiding understanding for our culture.

Indeed, many in our society are openly antagonistic towards the Christian understanding of the human person. They find the Christian teaching on certain matters like sexual identity, marriage and respect for life out of date or out of touch with contemporary values and are considered no longer acceptable. Indeed, it is not unusual these days for some people to be unable to understand how a reasonable person could possibly hold such views.

In the face of the dramatic change in our society's understanding of what it means to be human, there is a need to clearly articulate the Christian understanding. We could construct what could be called a Christian 'anthropological creed'.

Importance in education

In terms of the role of education, particularly Christian education, such a creed could become a very useful pedagogical tool both for parents and teachers alike. We cannot seek to educate the human person until we first understand and are able to clearly articulate who we are as human beings. Our approach to educational issues should be grounded in an authentically Christian anthropology. Such a clear formulation will assist in clarifying the distinctiveness of the Christian belief about the nature of the human person and so provide a sound foundation to our teaching. The goal of Christian formation is the human flourishing of the students we teach.

Loss of belief in God

The key influence in this changed understanding of the human person has been the loss of faith in God. In Western civilisation the human person has traditionally been understood in relation to the existence of God who created the universe and made human beings in his image and likeness, who calls human beings to relationship with Him on earth and offers eternal union with Him in heaven. Once God is removed from the equation, then each person is left to fashion their own self-understanding, often making their own self the centre of things. The loss of worship of God inevitably leads to a worship of self.

I will now explore some of the key elements of the Christian understanding of the human person. While many of these points may seem self-evident to us as Christians, we should be aware that for those outside a practicing Christian community they will seem quite foreign.

Indeed, as these Christian beliefs are expressed we could quietly consider someone we know – a friend or perhaps a family member - who is not a Christian and imagine their response to what is proposed.

The dignity of the human person

The Book of Genesis tells us that: 'God created man in his own image, in the image of God he created him, male and female he created them'[1].
Christians believe having been made in the image and likeness of God, each and every human being has an essential dignity and an intrinsic worth and value. Each human being matters.

The human being actually unites the spiritual and material worlds because each human being is a unity of a spiritual, immortal soul and a material body. The Second Vatican Council teaches that among all the creatures in the material world, only the human being is able to know and love God the Creator[2]. The human being, it says, is 'the only creature on earth that God has willed for its own sake[3]. Simply put, human beings are called to share in God's own life.

The *Catechism of the Catholic Church* explains the reason that the human being is a 'person' in these words:

> *Being in the image of God the human individual possesses the dignity of a person, who is not just something, but someone. He is capable of*

---

[1] Gen 1:27.
[2] *Gaudium et spes* (*GS*) 12.
[3] *GS* 24.

self-knowledge, of self-possession and of freely giving himself and entering into communion with other persons. And he is called by grace to a covenant with his Creator, to offer him a response of faith and love that no other creature can give in his stead[4].

The nature of the human person cannot be understood apart from a relationship with God.

A moral being

A critical part of being made in the image and likeness of God is that human beings have been endowed by God with the capacity to reason and are able to exercise free will[5]. It is through the exercise of reason and free will that the human person freely seeks and loves what is true and good. In his conscience, which is a judgment of his reason, the human person is able to recognise the voice of God urging him to do good and avoid evil[6].

God, in creating human beings with reason, allowed them through this reason to recognise and participate in the Divine Plan. This capacity, referred to as the Natural Law, gives human beings through the use of reason the capacity for true human flourishing[7].

The human person can find the law of God through the use of his reason and can live according to this law through the use of a properly formed conscience. This law is fulfilled in the love of God and of neighbour[8]. It is through having free will that the human person is morally responsibility for his own actions, and because of this he has the right to act in conscience and in freedom so as personally to make moral decisions. The human person has the obligation to inform

---

[4] CCC 357.
[5] Cf. CCC 1704.
[6] Cf. CCC 1778; *GS* 16.
[7] Cf. Thomas Aquinas, *Summa Theologiae* II Q 94.
[8] CCC 1706.

his conscience according to God's law with regard to moral action, and to form a right conscience[9].

Designed for marriage

The book of Genesis declares an important truth - that it is not good for man to be alone[10]. God created woman, the Book of Genesis says, as 'a helper fit for him'[11]. Man and woman are helpmates to each other and complement each other. Man and woman are equal in that they share in the same human nature, but do so in a complementary manner. They were designed to fulfil God's plan for creation: 'Be fruitful and multiply, and fill the earth and subdue it', the Book of Genesis declares[12].

Marriage is revealed as the union of one man and one woman, who 'become one flesh' in a nuptial union[13] so they can become procreators of life. This is the natural foundation for family life in which children, as a gift of God, are born and then nurtured in the loving and stable environment of the family.

All human beings are created as one of two possible sexes and therefore endowed with the gifts of either masculinity or femininity. Our sex as a man or woman is a constitutive element of being a human being. When human genetics is operating as it should our sex is established in and by our sex chromosomes. Our 23rd pair of chromosomes should either be XX, for a female or XY for a male. In a healthy properly functioning human body someone who has been created male cannot become a female, and vice versa, no matter

---

[9] CCC 1783-1785; cf. CCC 1849 and GS 16.
[10] Gen 2:18.
[11] Ibid.
[12] Gen 1:28.
[13] Gen 2:24.

what medical intervention they undertake to change their physical appearance[14].

The human body is a gift with a rich meaning. The call to communion is expressed in the physical difference and complementarity of man and woman. The Catholic Catechism teaches that 'physical, moral, and spiritual difference and complementarity are oriented toward the goods of marriage and the flourishing of family life. The harmony of the couple and of society depends in part on the way in which the complementarity, needs, and mutual support between the sexes are lived out'[15].

The Fall and Redemption

At the heart of the Christian understanding of the human condition is the account given in the Book of Genesis of the sin of Adam and Eve.

The first man and woman were created for divine intimacy. This intimate communion with God established harmony among our first parents and the rest of creation. But once this intimate communion with God was ruptured by sin, the grace of original holiness, as well as the harmony among our first parents and with all creation, was lost[16].

Sin is less an exercise of human freedom and more an abuse of that freedom[17]. It is disobedience towards God and a lack of trust in his goodness[18]. Sin is a pathology which is now part of the human condition. Human sin has both personal and social dimensions. Every sin is personal but is social in that it also has social repercussions[19].

---

[14] Cf. *Male and Female He created them*, Congregation for Catholic Education, 2019.
[15] CCC 2333-2334, see also 2361, 2372.
[16] Genesis 3, CCC 378-379.
[17] CCC 387.
[18] CCC 397.
[19] See CCC 408.

A CHRISTIAN ANTHROPOLOGICAL CREED

The Sacred Scriptures then recount the intention of God to redeem humanity now under the sway of sin. The supreme act of God to effect the redemption is found in the Incarnation and sacrificial death of Christ on Calvary.

God chose to redeem humanity because as St Paul taught, 'the wages of sin is death'[20]. The state of the human condition is such that we cannot save ourselves from sin and death[21]. God's way of redemption was to send his own Son to become a human being.

In Jesus, the incarnate Son of God, the true reality of being human is revealed. The Second Vatican Council states, 'In reality it is only in the mystery of the Word made flesh that the mystery of man truly becomes clear'[22].

In suffering and dying to ransom us from sin and death[23] Jesus Christ revealed the depths of his love for us and the extent to which he would go to reconcile us to himself[24]. In rising from the dead, Jesus Christ revealed the resurrected glory of body and soul to which we are called to share with God in heaven[25].

The Christian understands that he/she has been saved by Christ's death on the cross and in an act of faith embraces this saving grace. A Christian lives under the grace of the Holy Spirit poured out upon humanity which enables the Christian to live a life of virtue. As St Paul says, 'All I want is to be found in him, not having a righteousness of my own that comes from the law, but that which is through faith in Christ - the righteousness that comes from God on the basis of faith'[26]. As St Paul often says we are saved through faith, and not through works[27].

---

[20] Rom 6:23.
[21] CCC 389, 402-406.
[22] GS 22.
[23] Matt 20:28; 1 Jn 4:9-10; 4:14; 3:5; Jn 3:16.
[24] CCC 456-460.
[25] CCC 655; 1 Cor 15:20-22; Rom 8:11
[26] Phil 3:9.
[27] Eph 2:8-9.

However, we are also taught that we will be judged on our works. In the parable of the judgment of the nations, Jesus connects good works done in this life to the reward of heavenly joy[28]. Conversely, the omission of these same works is connected to eternal punishment.

The human person does not live as an isolated individual but in a communion of persons with interconnected relationships. The love of God is always connected to love of one's neighbour[29]. Consequently, the human person has responsibility for the wellbeing of others and should therefore seek the common good of society[30].

Destined for communion with God

The human person has a natural desire for happiness. Ultimately, this happiness is found in God alone[31]. The desire for God is written in the human heart as St Augustine famously wrote, 'You have made us for yourself [O Lord], and our heart is restless until it rests in you'[32]. The human person is called to union with God. The perfection of human nature is found in sharing God's own beatitude in heaven, in communion with all the angels and saints[33].

Although God calls each human person to share in his own divine life, which in turn resonates with the desire written in our hearts, each human person must respond freely to God's invitation. It is possible for individual human persons to reject or neglect God's call to share everlasting life with him[34].

---

[28] Mt 25:31-46.
[29] Mt 22:35-40, I Jn 4:20-21.
[30] CCC 1905-1912.
[31] GS 21.
[32] *Confessions* Bk 1 ch 1.
[33] Jn 17:3; 1 Cor 13:12; 1 Jn 3:2; Rev 7:9-10.
[34] CCC 29.

Christians believe that the great promise of salvation will be fulfilled in the resurrection of the body on the last day[35]. Immediately upon death, the immortal soul will receive Christ's particular judgment, and will await the time when it will be reunited with its body in the general resurrection of the dead[36]. The immortal soul will be reunited with its body when Christ returns in glory on the day of the resurrection of the dead[37]. The righteous human person, body and soul, will share in heavenly beatitude in Christ's kingdom; while the unrighteous human person, body and soul, will receive eternal punishment.

Living in Society - Human Rights and Responsibilities

One final point needs to be made in relation to the fundamental rights and responsibilities of every human person that flow from their human dignity and God's Law. The Catholic faith, based on divine revelation and human reason illuminated by faith, has consequences for human rights and responsibilities.

Gaudium et Spes teaches that 'there is a growing awareness of the exalted dignity proper to the human person, since he stands above all things, and his rights and duties are universal and inviolable'[38]. These rights and duties have been articulated in a number of the social encyclicals[39].

The Church has consistently spoken of the fundamental right to life. Every new human life is precious in the eyes of the Lord. The Catholic Catechism teaches: 'From its conception, the child has the right to life'[40]. The Church has also consistently defended the rights of the sick, the

---

[35] CCC 997-998; Jn 5:29; cf. Dan 12:2; Matt 25:31-46.
[36] CCC 1021-1022.
[37] CCC 1005.
[38] GS 26
[39] E.g. *Centesimus Annus* 47.
[40] CCC 2322.

handicapped, the suffering and the aged[41]. Because of the intrinsic dignity of the human person, every human life must be protected from conception to natural death. In the light of the passion of Christ, suffering is redemptive if accepted in union with Christ's passion and death[42].

There is a mutual complementarity in the Church's understanding of rights and responsibilities among men and women as both flow from the moral law and ultimately the Law of God. Both rights and responsibilities are ways of expressing the moral law, which itself is the expression of what is required for human flourishing. Of course, we find the most fundamental list of our duties in the Ten Commandments.

It is because we have a duty to seek and know the truth that the Church maintains that each human person has the right to pursue the truth in freedom, hence it recognises importance of freedom of a properly formed conscience and freedom of religion. The Church however has the responsibility to help the human person form his or her conscience rightly according to the moral law and present the truth to each person so that they might know it.

Governments have the critical and difficult role of both promoting the truth of the human person and their flourishing but also ensuring citizens have the freedom to pursue the truth, particularly what they believe to be the truth in the light of their own conscientiously held beliefs.

Human freedom is not absolute as though the human person were able to determine the moral law according to their own lights. Rather, human freedom arises from our dignity in being created in God's image.

Credal Statements

Thus, at this point, can we assemble a Christian Anthropological Creed? That is, in the light of our reflection on the nature of the human person given to us from both

---

[41] CCC 2276.
[42] Col 1:24.

human reason and divine revelation, can we express a set of beliefs which provide the principles upon which we as individual Christians can base our lives. These principles are then the inspiration for our life in human society. They are also the source of our promotion of the good of the human person within society.

I propose the following as a possible Christian anthropological creed:

We believe the human person is made in the image of God, has been redeemed by the passion and death of Jesus Christ, and is called to share eternal life with God in heaven.

As a consequence, the human person has inherent dignity which cannot be understood apart from our relationship with God.

We believe all people form the unity of the human race by reason of the common origin which they have from God.

We believe man and woman have been created by God in equal dignity insofar as they are human persons. At the same time, they have been created in a reciprocal complementarity insofar as they are masculine and feminine.

We believe that masculinity and femininity are gifts from God which are embraced and not altered or changed.

We believe men and women are called to subdue the earth as good 'stewards' of what God has created.

We believe the human person, created by God, is a union of a body and a spiritual, immortal soul. This soul does not perish when it separates from the body at death, and will be reunited with its body at the final Resurrection.

We believe the human person has reason and free will, capable of understanding the order of creation and of making moral decisions. The human person is responsible for his or her own free actions.

We believe the human person has freedom to act according to the laws determined by God as the way to attain happiness. This freedom is not absolute but relative insofar as it is related to, and dependent upon, God himself.

We believe the human person has the right to freedom of conscience and freedom of religion. Within the society, the Church has the responsibility to help the human person form his or her conscience rightly according to the natural moral law and the Gospel.

We believe the human person has the right to life, which is to be protected from conception to natural death.

We believe the human person inherits the effects of original sin and human nature, without being totally corrupted, is wounded in its natural powers.

We believe that in his Incarnation Jesus Christ came to redeem humanity from sin and death.

We believe that the marriage covenant, by which one man and one woman form with each other an intimate communion of life and love, has been founded and endowed with its own special laws by the Creator.

We believe that by its very nature marriage is ordered to the good of the couple, as well as to the generation and education of children. We believe Christ the Lord raised marriage between the baptised to the dignity of a sacrament.

We believe the child has the right to be conceived in a conjugal union of their own natural mother and father, and to be raised by them.

We believe that every human person is to be accorded the respect due to their dignity of being made in the image of God, redeemed by Christ, and called to intimate communion with God.

Conclusion

A creed provides a set of beliefs. Just was the Christian tradition produced creeds to outline its belief about the nature of God, so, in our time, there is a need to develop a set of beliefs which provide an understanding of what Christians believe about the nature of the human person.

We could call this a 'Christian manifesto' or a 'Statement of Beliefs', but the use of creeds in Christian history, offers us a way of describing what we believe as Christians about the nature of the human person.

For a young people to be able to grow to healthy human maturity they need to be formed and educated on the basis of the Christian understanding of the nature of the human person.

GOVERNOR BOURKE'S VISION AND ITS CURRENT FRUIT IN GOVERNMENT SCHOOL RELIGIOUS EDUCATION

Peter Robinson

Last year on 20 February former Chief Justice of Australia, the Hon. Michael Kirby, gave the address at the annual speech day of his old school, Fort Street High School, Australia's oldest public high school.[1]

Kirby's speech was mainly about his understanding of the meaning of the word 'secular' in the NSW Education Acts from the 19th century and why he saw Governor Richard Bourke (1831-37) as a 'Sentinel of Secularism', the champion of the secularisation of public education in eastern Australia. Given its definitive form in the 1880 Education Act of New South Wales, building on the earlier legislation of 1848 and 1866, at that point public education was described as 'compulsory, free and secular', the official description that continues to the present. But public education in New South Wales has been officially defined since the 19th century as 'secular' in the sense of 'non-sectarian, not non-religious'[2]. It

---

[1] The Hon. Michael Kirby, *Sentinels of Secularism*, Fort Street High School Annual Speech Day Address, Sydney Town Hall, 21 February 2020.

[2] NSW Education Act 1990 Section 30: 'Secular Instruction. In government schools, the education is to consist of strictly non-

does not mean an absence of religion which is what many now take 'secular' to mean. This seriously confuses a lot of people. We find it hard after over a century of vigorous promotion of *secularism* (the word, though not the idea, first coined in 1851 to mean the absence of the sacred or religion from public life) to realise that in the history of its use 'secular' (Latin: *saeculum*) arose as a Christian theological word, originating in the early 5th century with St. Augustine in his magisterial work *The City of God*. The *saeculum* there is the present age in which both the City of Man and the City of God co-exist, though in continual tension until the Day of Judgement and the end of this world, making way for the New Heavens and the New Earth in which righteousness dwells. In this sense nothing on earth is outside the *saeculum* until that time.[3]

He might be surprised at my objection to his definition of secular because significant historians have promoted the view he espouses. Kirby portrays himself and his student hearers as Sentinels of Secularism, taking their inspiration from Governor Bourke and his vision for public education. But research in the last couple of decades has exposed the misleading use of Bourke's role in the development of modern Australia by Hegelian historians to serve their secularisation narrative.[4]

---

sectarian and secular instruction. The words "secular instruction" are to be taken to include general religious education as distinct from dogmatic or polemical theology.' Note that the new Section 33A re. special education in ethics uses 'secular' contrary to the meaning above, as it excludes any ethics education based on religious sources delivered non-dogmatically.

[3] R. A. Markus: *Saeculum: History and Society in the Theology of St. Augustine*, Cambridge University Press 1970, pp. 16, 20.
[4] Hastie, David: 'The Latest Installment in the Whig Interpretation of Australian Education History: Catherine Byrne's *JORH* Article 'Free, Complulsory and (not) Secular'', *Journal of Religious History* 41:3 (September 2017) 386-403.

Before moving to the fruit of Governor Bourke's promotion of the Irish National Schools System for Eastern Australia, what was the foundation Bourke laid? And if it wasn't secularist, what was it?

Bourke the Misrepresented

Major General Sir Richard Bourke of County Limerick was regarded by former Prime Minister Gough Whitlam (1972-75) as one of the Big Four of the colonial governors of NSW. But historian Max Waugh calls him the *Forgotten Hero*, while also regarding him as the leading social reformer in Australia in the 19th century.[5] Bourke has been misunderstood or misrepresented by major Australian historians. Ward's *Australian Legend* and Manning Clark's *History of Australia* both fail to account for the impact of Bourke's most deeply held spiritual convictions and his strong desire to apply in Eastern Australia his vision for civic life built on common Christian belief and morality to discourage the extreme religious sectarianism between Protestant and Catholic that he knew all too well in his native Ireland. The impact of his far-seeing vision can still be discerned in many of the assumptions and social values of 21st century Australia. He had a clear vision for a cohesive society largely built on common beliefs and morals shared by the (at least nominally) mostly Christian population.

---

[5] Whitlam's Forward p. xi in Waugh, Max: *Forgotten Hero. Richard Bourke, Irish-born Governor of New South Wales 1831-1837*, Australian Scholarly Publishing, Melbourne 2005; also, Waugh p. xvii. The other three governors he names are Phillip, Macquarie and Gipps.

Above: Governor Bourke's 1842 statue outside the State Library of NSW.
Below: Memorial plaque for Elizabeth Bourke in St. John's, Parramatta

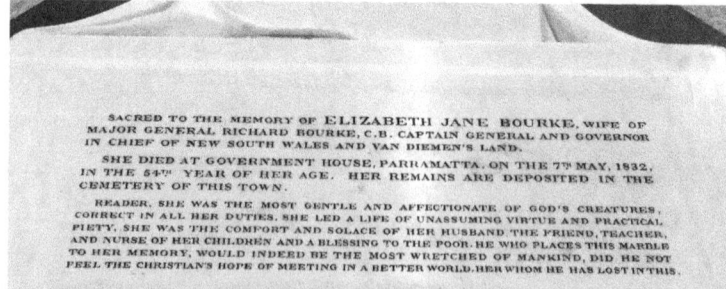

SACRED TO THE MEMORY OF ELIZABETH JANE BOURKE, WIFE OF MAJOR GENERAL RICHARD BOURKE, C.B. CAPTAIN GENERAL AND GOVERNOR IN CHIEF OF NEW SOUTH WALES AND VAN DIEMEN'S LAND.

SHE DIED AT GOVERNMENT HOUSE, PARRAMATTA, ON THE 7TH MAY, 1832, IN THE 54TH YEAR OF HER AGE. HER REMAINS ARE DEPOSITED IN THE CEMETERY OF THIS TOWN.

READER, SHE WAS THE MOST GENTLE AND AFFECTIONATE OF GOD'S CREATURES, CORRECT IN ALL HER DUTIES. SHE LED A LIFE OF UNASSUMING VIRTUE AND PRACTICAL PIETY. SHE WAS THE COMFORT AND SOLACE OF HER HUSBAND THE FRIEND, TEACHER, AND NURSE OF HER CHILDREN AND A BLESSING TO THE POOR. HE WHO PLACES THIS MARBLE TO HER MEMORY, WOULD INDEED BE THE MOST WRETCHED OF MANKIND, DID HE NOT FEEL THE CHRISTIAN'S HOPE OF MEETING IN A BETTER WORLD, HER WHOM HE HAS LOST IN THIS.

Bourke's Achievements

Soon after his arrival in December 1831 Bourke identified the expansion of churches and schools, as well as economic, judicial and political reforms to be important for preparing NSW for the development of settler society post convict transportation. Fundamental to his proposed church and school reforms was his own experience of society and politics in Ireland and particularly in County Limerick in the 1820s, as well as his own drive to expand shared Trinitarian Christian belief. He gained approval for his reforms from the Whig government in London by 1835, 'when a group of devout liberal Anglicans [like Bourke himself] who became dominant in the Whig government, gave the Evangelicals in the Colonial Office support to approve Bourke's plan.'[6]

His achievements as governor were considerable despite strong opposition to some of his policies. He was forward-thinking with his brief to prepare Eastern Australia for the development of a culture on which Australian civilisation could be built beyond the end of transportation in 1842, which envisaged a great increase in immigration from Great Britain. To start facilitating this he improved the selection standards for migrants, and inaugurated assisted immigration, including a bounty system to repay settlers who brought out workers and their families for specific jobs. He already had experience with assisted migration in Ireland and in South Africa. The colonial population more than doubled over his time as governor, and around the time of his

---

[6] David Stoneman: *The Church Act: the expansion of Christianity or the imposition of moral enlightenment?* PhD University of New England 2011, p. 321.

departure the 'free' population outnumbered the 'convict' population.[7]

From the beginning Bourke insisted on more humane treatment of convicts, which earned him enemies amongst many landholders who relied on large numbers of assigned convicts but often treated them badly. He also limited the powers of magistrates to make them more accountable in their dealing with convicts. The governor's actions brought many abusive landholders to justice.[8] He established a savings bank for convicts to protect their money while finishing their sentences. Prior to that many never saw their possessions again. He restored full civic rights for emancipists including holding public office as Macquarie had done twenty years earlier. So, when he introduced trial by jury for civil trials for the first time, he permitted emancipists to do jury duty.[9]

The governor insisted strongly on respect for the indigenous population and took an active interest in their welfare, and key supporters of his backed legal action over the Myall Creek Massacre the year after he left.[10] Bourke encouraged legal expansion of settlement beyond the Nineteen Counties, with the Squatting Act of 1836. With a keen eye on the longer-term development of Australia he declared the settlement on Port Phillip by Batman and associates for which Governor Arthur in Tasmania sought jurisdiction - much to Bourke's fury, and London's refusal - to be illegal, and as Governor-in-Chief, formally established Melbourne under the crown. He named the settlement and its first streets and oversaw the street plan.[11]

---

[7] Max Waugh: *Forgotten Hero. Richard Bourke, Irish-born Governor of New South Wales 1831-1837*, Australian Scholarly Publishing, Melbourne 2005, pp. 53, 103
[8] Waugh, op.cit., pp. 58-61.
[9] Ibid., pp. 52f, 125-31.
[10] Ibid., pp. 133-41, 185, 191.
[11] Ibid., pp. 107-121

Bourke insisted on a free press, despite the enormous damage done to him in the press himself, as it gave free voice to his most virulent critics. Despite this, he stuck to his principles. He also prepared the way for elected representation in the Legislative Council of NSW, looking forward to eventual full democratic government.[12]

Public Education

In 1836 Bourke attempted unsuccessfully to establish public education based on the Irish National Schools system. Fundamental to this proposal was the idea developed in Ireland from the 1790s to encourage a sense of shared Christian beliefs and morals in state-run public schools to discourage sectarian conflict by offering General Religious Instruction in core shared beliefs of the Christian faith approved by denominational heads, while giving full recognition to the distinctive emphases of each denomination for their students by also having Special Religious Instruction delivered by the clergy or their representatives.[13]

As was the Irish Whig intention, Bourke expected this would give expression to religious freedom and reduce sectarian conflict in NSW. He was deeply disappointed at its rejection. But his proposal did not die and supporters in the NSW legislature succeeded in enacting legislation in 1848, eleven years after his departure, to be followed by the Education Acts of 1866, 1880 and those up to 1990. It was also the foundation for public education in the soon independent colonies of Victoria and Queensland and influenced the other colonies.[14]

So, despite the rebuttal, public education in Australia would be one of the most enduring legacies of Bourke's governorship. This legacy came directly out of his experience

---

[12] Ibid., p. 191.
[13] Ibid., pp. 76-85
[14] Ibid., pp. 86-93.

in Ireland where he had been involved in the development of the Irish system. He also had 'skin in the game' as a landholder with the children of his Catholic tenant farmers for whom he and his wife Elizabeth built a schoolhouse for 79 students in 1820, before the new Irish system began, employing the teachers, setting minimal fees for the families, and subsidising those who couldn't afford them. They even provided the Catholic Douay Bible for their use.[15]

The Church Act 1836.

Also important for this paper, in addition to the Catholic Emancipation Act in Britain in 1829, in 1836, in religious terms, Governor Bourke enfranchised the Catholic, Presbyterian and Methodist populations alongside the majority Church of England through the NSW Church Act of 1836 and its successors across the colonies. This prepared the way for other non-conformist - and eventually even Jewish – populations to be included. The Church Act is regarded by Waugh as the most significant Australian social legislation of the 19th century.[16]

The Church Act greatly boosted civic development in communities across all six colonies, with similar legislation, by giving proportional funding for new churches, land for schools, and clergy stipends, which was taken up with great enthusiasm and appreciation, even, in the end, by the Church of England who benefitted far more than they would have if they had succeeded in gaining formal recognition as *the* Established Church. But state support was withdrawn in all colonies in the 1860s, effectively secularising[17] Australian

---

[15] Ibid., p. 17.
[16] Ibid., pp. 85-6.
[17] In the traditional sense preserved in the NSW Education Acts, of non-sectarian in regard to government institutions, but not non-religious as regards the public exercise and influence of religion in society, resulting in the publicly pluralist culture of modern

society. However, by this time these acts had had an extraordinary effect on the growth of civic life across settled Australia, and through the rest of the century, well fulfilling Bourke's brief to prepare for the development of settler society post-transportation. It was a truly nation-building initiative well before federation. The four or so churches in nearly every town established before the end of the 19th century across Australia are the spiritual, physical and symbolic evidence of how Australia was so quickly transformed from a few mostly convict colonies in the 1830s into the most prosperous and possibly democratically advanced country per capita on earth by the early 1900s.[18]

Bourke's Legacy

Bourke's legacy can be summed up in these distinct achievements, begun or planned in the face of frequent opposition from entrenched interests. He realised that the churches were the key to developing a cohesive civilisation in eastern Australia. He was encouraged in this by his reforming Whig friends in the British government. He wanted to overcome the sectarian competition between denominations, and to enfranchise Catholics in particular. He may have succeeded more than we are used to recognising, according to Stuart Piggin and Robert Linder, with their description of 'holy emulation' [19] between denominations in communities across the country outdoing each other in building church infrastructure, rather than being solely focussed on the sectarian conflict narrative of Ireland and Britain which climaxed the 1890s and which has

---

Australia. There has never been a 'wall of separation' between church and state in Australia. That is not Australia's story.
[18] Stuart Piggin and Robert Linder, *The Fountain of Public Prosperity*, Volume 1 of *Evangelicals in Australian History (1740-1914)* Monash University Publishing 2018, pp. 256-8; 272, 3.
[19] Ibid., p. 273.

been to some extent too much read back into Irish history in the 1820s and into Bourke's NSW in the 1830s.[20]

The Outcome for Public Education

But Bourke would have been dismayed to see how the immoderate sectarianism he knew in the newspapers of Sydney (the social media of the day whose freedom, ironically, he championed) hugely fuelled later by the escalating sectarian conflicts in Ireland mid- to late-century, almost succeeded in scuttling his dream of an effective public education system that would help establish civilisation in Australia based on common Christian belief and practice. If anything, the Irish National Schools system in NSW became a catalyst for the expression of sectarian tribalism in the arguments focused on the 1848, 1866 and 1880 parliamentary debates, and as we know, the Catholic Church chose to rely its own school system, while several Protestant associations sought to leverage public education to marginalise the Catholic population and influence. Leading up to the 1880 Act a proportion of the Protestant population, much to the distress of other Protestants, supported the loss of funding for their own denominational schools, and hence the demise of most, if that's what it took to force Catholics schools to close.[21]

The Church of England social reformer Archdeacon Francis Bertie Boyce who had been a key advocate for the continuation of state funding for denominational schools at that time considered it to be less a disaster than a compromise when reflecting on those events years later: 'State aid was withdrawn from the denominational schools, but religious instruction was kept as part of the curriculum

---

[20] Jennifer Ridden: 'The Forgotten History of the Protestant Crusade: Religious Liberalism in Ireland', *Journal of Religious History* 31:1 (March 2007) pp. 101, 2.
[21] Robert Withycombe, *Bertie Boyce: Pioneer Clergyman, Social Reformer*, Morning Star Publishing, Reservoir Victoria, 2018, p. 24.

of the State schools.' His final appraisal was: 'After 50 years trial of the new system, I still believe that the State was unwise to withdraw its aid from the denominational schools. One great section of the community, the Roman Catholics, feels itself injured, in that it contributed to the cost of the State educational system, and also has to provide schools for its own children without assistance from the State. I believe, too, that had nothing been done to combat the wave of secularism, every vestige of religious training would have been swept from our educational system.'[22] As it was, Premier Sir Henry Parkes's measure to preserve the right of Religious Instruction in the 1880 Act was carried by only four votes.

Bourke's Departure

Bourke decided to leave NSW a year early at the end of 1837 after some bruising episodes exacerbated by the free press he was so committed to. The enfranchising of Catholics in NSW earned him the gratitude and affection of much of the Irish Catholic population who were very well represented among the many thousands gathered at his departure from Government House in Bridge Street and then by the harbour.[23] They were also highly represented among those who generously subscribed funds for the statue erected in his honour five years later, now outside the Public Library of NSW, the first civic statue erected in Australia.[24] It states, among his many achievements, that 'He established religious equality on a just and firm basis and sought to provide for all, without distinction of sect, a sound and adequate system of national education.'[25]

---

[22] Ibid., pp. 24, 25.
[23] Waugh op. cit., pp. 162, 4.
[24] Ibid., pp. 165-72.
[25] Ibid., p. 169.

But who was Richard Bourke?

Landed gentry from Limerick, the Bourkes traced their heritage back to the Norman line of de Burghs who arrived in Ireland in the 12th century. It is said the Norman gentry became more Irish than the Irish. By the time of Richard's birth in 1777 his family was facing testing times as his father was an inveterate gambler who lost most of his estate. His mother sought to remove Richard from his father's influence as much as possible. At the age of six Richard was sent to Westminster School in London, his father's old school.

He was also under the regular care of their distant cousin, politician and political thinker Sir Edmund Burke and his wife Jane at Beaconsfield outside London during many of his vacations all through his schooling and then at Oxford, continuing to visit Mrs Burke after Edmund's death in 1797. She had been like a foster mother to him, and Sir Edmund was certainly his mentor growing up. The influence of the Burkes was deep and long-lasting. Richard was deeply impressed by the Burkes' mixed Protestant and Catholic marriage. In his retirement Richard co-edited Sir Edmund's many volumes of correspondence.[26]

Through the Burkes he was also formally introduced to English-born Elizabeth Bourke, whose father John was a close friend of Sir Edmund, and brother a fellow-student of Richard's at Westminster. Elizabeth already had a reputation for philanthropy as a young woman. They were blessed with a very loving marriage. Five of their eight children survived into adulthood. Richard and Elizabeth were both Anglican/Church of Ireland, and they shared a deep credally orthodox Christian faith, he an ecclesiastically liberal high churchman, and she an evangelical. They combined well in matters of faith and social concern. English by birth of Irish descent and born a Bourke herself, Richard could rely on Elizabeth for support in his most compelling interests.

---

[26] Ibid., pp. 1-3.

Waugh notes, 'Bourke's deep and enduring love for his wife and their children became the hallmark of his life.'[27]

After graduating from Oxford where he attended Oriel College, then after his father died, Exeter College, he sought a commission in the army in late 1798 after some brief legal experience. For sixteen years had a distinguished military career during the Napoleonic Wars. Early on he was scarred for life in the Netherlands on 6 October, 1799 when shot in the jaw fighting at close quarters, one of over 500 British casualties in that engagement.[28]

Bourke had invaluable experience for his future role in NSW when he was asked to take over as Acting Governor of Cape Colony (1826-28). While there he showed his commitment to addressing injustices suffered by the natives and ordered that coloured domestic slaves be engaged as paid servants and he made other significant improvements to the relations between blacks and whites, measures nonetheless reversed by his successor. He was even-handed in helping promote mission work by different churches among the tribes.[29]

By the time he arrived in Sydney he was a major general. Accepting the post of Governor of NSW, Bourke arrived in Sydney on the brig *Margaret* on December 3, 1831, with Elizabeth and three of their grown children. They hoped that coming to NSW would help Elizabeth's increasingly poor health. But the rough voyage left her desperately weak. Five months later she died suddenly at Government House, Parramatta, aged 53. Elizabeth had always been a true companion and strength to him. With a well-deserved reputation for helping the disadvantaged, in a letter to her daughter Fanny in Ireland not long before she died Elizabeth was anxious to hear of someone 'taking an interest in the poor near Thornfield.'[30]

---

[27] Ibid., p. 4.
[28] Ibid..
[29] Ibid., pp. 32, 29.
[30] Ibid., pp. 46, 47.

Bourke erected a moving tribute to her in St. John's Church of England, Parramatta, which reflected their shared confidence in the reality of the resurrection.[31]

A High Church Liberal in Limerick

Richard and Elizabeth Bourke were strongly connected in the British Whig establishment. Jennifer Ridden's 2007 article on Religious Liberalism in Ireland, which especially focusses on the Whig gentry of Limerick in the 1820s, and the networks of these mixed denomination families is particularly illuminating about the conditions that prepared Bourke for his role in NSW.

They were already used to standing up to fellow gentry as they sought to improve the conditions for impoverished Catholics in Limerick. They were as committed to the enfranchising of Catholics in Ireland as they were to be in NSW.

While clearly Protestant and committed to Christian missions they were nevertheless strongly opposed to the behaviour and impact of the Second Reformation Movement in Ireland from 1815 which was often insensitive about the impact of the political power imbalance between Protestants and Catholics when aggressively proselytising the latter, and the movement was a significant irritant in the worsening relations there between Catholic and Protestant.

Ridden highlights the different reactions of Protestants to the largely lay Second Reformation Movement. She gives evidence for the backlash of some influential Protestants that was quite the opposite of the growing binary sectarian conflict. 'In County Limerick, for example, two versions of Church of Ireland opposition to the Second Reformation Movement emerged during 1820, among high church clergy, including Bishop Jebb, and among liberal Protestant gentlemen. Instead of closing down debate into rigid binary

---

[31] Bourke's attitude to his mother's death the previous year was the same. Stonehouse op. cit., p. 348.

opposition along sectarian lines, the Limerick evidence shows that the Crusade produced a much more complex religious, social and political debate than historians have recognised, which, in turn, made possible a wider range of responses to key Irish problems.'[32] Bourke was one such very well-connected gentleman, and his daughter Fanny was to marry Bishop Jebb's nephew, Rev. John Jebb.

Athamik

It is also now recognised that a substantial political pamphlet under the name 'Athamik' written that year in response to Bishop Mant of Killaloe's intolerant inaugural sermon as bishop, was in fact written by Richard Bourke. So, we now need have no doubt about his social and spiritual vision for Ireland. We know what his motivations were, why they were not an expression of secularisation, but a vision of a society based on a biblically orthodox and credally faithful conception of common Christianity, forged in the intense societal and political tensions of Ireland in the 25 years after the Napoleonic Wars, with roots back into the 1790s. As Athamik, Bourke wrote, 'But while there is a sense, and a most important one, in which the Protestant is exclusively our Established Church, there is another, and not an unimportant sense, in which the Roman Catholic also is, in Ireland, *an* Established Church. If that be established, which the law allows, acknowledges and protects - then is the Roman Catholic an Established Church among us.'[33] When appointed to NSW he had the opportunity to apply much of that vision to this colonial proving ground, plural establishment in particular, despite the eventual failure of those who sought a plural establishment in Ireland itself.[34]

---

[32] Ridden op. cit. *Abstract* p. 78.
[33] Athamik *Letter*, p. 7 quoted in ibid., p. 96.
[34] Ibid., p. 97.

The Secularisation Myth

In short, the evidence of historians Jennifer Ridden and David Stonehouse shows conclusively that Bourke was no liberal seculariser or Enlightenment rationalist. But Michael Roe, Manning Clark, Russell Ward and Allan Grocott, for instance, all depict the Church Acts as inherently secularist, providing social control by the moral police for 'moral enlightenment'. In short, they see the Church Acts as 'a manifestation of anticlericalism and indifference to religion, both marks of the secular[35] mind'.[36] Nothing could be further from the truth.

Theirs has been just another example of what Piggin and Linder have drawn attention to as a chronically stereotyped interpretation of Australian religious history, 'that Australia is a secular nation and that its Christianity has been sectarian.'[37] They observe that studies of the Church Acts 1836/9 in NSW typically perpetuate these stereotypes. Their thesis is that the Church Acts were designed to increase rather than diminish the role of religion in public policy, 'that instead of creating or abolishing a Church of England Establishment they created a plural establishment of the mainstream Christian denominations which greatly increased the capacity of churches to influence Australian values, and that it represented, not the separation, but the complementarity of church and state in the interest of community development.'[38]

Ridden concludes her article with the observation that the political and ecclesiastical liberals Bourke belonged to in Limerick who were seeking to combat the escalating sectarian conflict were also 'afraid of an unrestrained rights-based Enlightenment discourse, which they thought would

---

[35] [ist] is added to clarify that 'secular' is used here to mean secularist. See p. 1, paragraph 2 above.
[36] Piggin & Linder op. cit., pp. 253, 4.
[37] Ibid., p. 251.
[38] Ibid..

produce the revolutionary excesses that had characterised 1798 [in Ireland] and which continued to characterise revolutionary France. Instead, they looked to the state to facilitate what we would today call a 'civil society', whose key values were Christian and latitudinarian; neither sectarian nor secular.'[39]

Richard Bourke shared his mentor Edmund Burke's horror at the dismantling or repression of so many of France's cultural and spiritual institutions during the revolution, and his Church Act expressed his desire to elevate the sources of a truly just and Christianised society, and not at all to marginalise them. His conflict with those who wanted the churches, especially those under the Church of England to control all education was not because he saw his preferred system as simply replacing the church schools as Kirby thinks. Bourke had a more holistic view of integrating the contribution of the churches into the heart of the emerging culture of eastern Australia through public schooling.

As is seen in the Athamik pamphlet Bourke was going out of his way to resist the emerging possibility of secularisation in his French Revolution-impacted world. Political debate about the French Revolution involving his mentor Edmund Burke was very likely a significant element in conversations at Beaconsfield. Sir Edmund's influential book, *Reflections on the Revolution in France* was published in 1791 the year Richard turned fourteen. The fraught issues of the Revolution were affecting relations among the Whigs in parliament, and they dominated much of Edmund Burke's work over his last few years while Richard was finishing at Westminster and then at Oxford, in close reach of Beaconsfield during this most impressionable time in his formation. His great mentor died in July 1797 the year Richard turned twenty. He had no reason to differ significantly from Sir Edmund's view of the French upheaval, and while in NSW Bourke had a copy of

---

[39] Ridden Op. Cit. p. 102, also quoted in Ibid p. 254

Lord John Russell's *Causes of the French Revolution* that he left with his daughter Anne and son-in-law Edward Deas Thomson, Colonial Secretary of NSW, which mirrored Bourke's own statements in his Athamik pamphlet.[40]

Into the Present

A minority of Catholic parents sent their children to public schools from the beginning of public education across Australia despite the strong promotion by Catholic clergy of their own denominational system and official rejection of the public system. Catholic parents were increasingly likely to send their children to their local public school from the middle of the 20th century onwards, even though already by the time of WW1 up to 40% of Catholic children were attending public schools in NSW.[41] The 1960s saw very rapid growth in the number of Catholic students in public schools in NSW, doubling between 1960 and 1970. This was the continuation of the post-war baby-boom as well as of strong Catholic immigration from the late 1940s onwards when the Catholic proportion of the population relative to the total Christian population significantly increased. Ann Maree Whenman's assessment is that 'the growth in that age sector of the population, the number of students staying longer in school, and the inability of Catholic Secondary schools to accommodate all the Catholic secondary school age students,' were also reasons for the increase in the 1960s.[42]

By 2001 the proportion of all Catholic students across Australia in the different school types were government schools 43%, other non-government schools 5% and

---

[40] Stoneman *op. cit.* pp. 353,4; Athamik *Letter,* p. 40 passim; Waugh op. cit., p. 48.
[41] Ann Maree Whenman: *In Good Faith: A historical study of the provision of religious education for Catholic children not in Catholic Schools in New South Wales. The CCD Movement 1880-2000.* ACU PhD, July 2011, p. 51
[42] Ibid., pp. 173-4; 181-3; 215.

Catholic schools 52%.[43] By 2020 there were more Catholic students in government schools than Catholic schools. Another feature worth noting is the 'bleeding' between schooling systems in terms of denominational and faith alignment. For instance, in 2018 the proportion of non-Catholic students in Australian Catholic schools was 34%. In NSW it was 29.1%, more than half of which was other Christian denominations.[44]

Since 1960 with the rejuvenation of the Confraternity for Christian Doctrine (CCD) Catholic dioceses in NSW have been increasingly supportive of and effective in delivering SRE for Catholic students in NSW and have for some years had more SRE teachers registered in NSW than all other Christian denominations combined, though joint-Protestant Scripture classes have generally been larger than Catholic classes. In her 2011 PhD on Catholic SRI/SRE 1880-2000 where she documents the changes in the proportion of Catholic students in public schools in NSW and the development of Catholic SRI/SRE, Whenman remarks that at a meeting in 1969 'the Chairman of the NSW Council for Christian Education in Schools (CCES), Canon Alan Langdon, recalled first becoming aware 'of the existence, let alone the work of the CCD'. Langdon observed 'it seems incredible' that 'a movement of such great significance for special religious education in NSW: the establishment of the Confraternity of Christian Doctrine (CCD) in 1960' was not known to the members of CCES.'[45]

It was from the late 1960s that Alan Langdon, who was the head of the Anglican Diocese of Sydney Department of Education, took seriously Director General Harold

---

[43] *National Catholic Education Commission (NCEC) RE Committee* (2006), in ibid. p. 278.
[44] *NCEC Report 2019*, pp. 14-15.
[45] Whenman op. cit., p. 242. See also Langdon, A. A.: 'Religious Education in the Public (Government) Schools of New South Wales: Part II: Special Religious Education.' *Journal of Christian Education*, 35(2) (1992), p. 11.

Wyndham's [46] plea to form an SRE peak body for the churches, and through his initiative and inter-denominational cooperation in 1972 the Inter-Church Commission on Religious Education in Schools (ICCOREIS) was formed.[47]

We are at a critical juncture for the future of SRE and GRE in Australia. The elephant in the room is not the old British Isles-derived sectarianism. It is multiculturalism. It is getting harder for secularists to ignore the importance of religion in the lives of a significant proportion of newer arrivals in Australia from diverse backgrounds. The Christchurch massacre has put the wind up Australian governments. There is significant interest from politicians and departments of education in what should be done with General Religious Education, the almost defunct element from the Irish model, required by the NSW Act but seriously under-offered by most public schools in NSW since the 1960s. Meanwhile those working hard to make SRE effective contend with very patchy administration of SRE by too many school executives, and campaigns against it by organised principals and the NSW Teachers Federation. Even so, both sides of politics in NSW have made clear reaffirmations of the importance of SRE over the last decade, which can't be said of Victoria. Queensland in 2018 saw the formation of both an all-faiths peak body and a combined churches peak body, the first such bodies since the successful referendum to reintroduce religious education to Queensland state schools in 1910.

New Research and Perspective for the Future

Of immediate significance is research by Zehavit Gross from the School of Education at Bar Ilan University, Israel, and Suzanne Rutland from the Department of Hebrew, Biblical and Jewish Studies at Sydney University into the fit-

---

[46] Sir Harold Wyndham, Director General of Education 1952-68.
[47] ICCOREIS, established in 1972, was preceded by the Council for Christian Education in Schools (CCES).

for-purpose potential of GRE and SRE in Australian public education. They have recommended that teaching about beliefs and values common to the world's great religions be reinforced through a revamped GRE,[48] maintaining faith-specific teaching through SRE taught by qualified adherents, while undertaking a more thoroughgoing review of the pedagogy of both aspects of religious education.[49] This is a serious piece of academic research relating to a major issue of concern in Australian society, and deserves to be taken up by state and territory education departments in thinking through their responsibilities under their various education acts towards the children of different faith communities, and to understand better the importance of the role of religion and belief in society. Far from becoming defunct, Gross and

---

[48] Current GRE, especially in NSW, is really beyond the scope of this paper given the way it has both suffered systemic neglect and been significantly modified due to the very different make-up of the Australian community since the second half of the C20th. Those claiming a Christian affiliation currently are proportionally about half what they were around 1901, even though remaining by far the largest religion and the one most influential in shaping the culture of modern Australia. If Gross and Rutland's recommendations are seriously taken up there is the challenge for the churches to be fully engaged in conversations with education departments and other religions about how to adapt the provision of GRE from its original purpose. That purpose was to teach common Christianity and core Bible passages to students from the whole range of Christian denominations. Giving students insight into the range of different religions held by the families of their classmates in schools and communities with a diverse religious make up - and none - with the aim of developing genuine understanding of that diversity, as well as commonly held ideas and morals, is a worthy if challenging aim for social cohesion. The effective use of GRE should attract serious engagement in the near future given the recent (2021) release of Gross and Rutland's full research report and recommendations:
[49] Zehavit Gross and Suzanne D. Rutland: *Special Religious Education in Australia and its Value to Contemporary Society*, Springer, Cham Switzerland 2021.

Rutland have shown that SRE and GRE have significant implications and potential both nationally and globally.[50]

Richard Bourke also had a remarkable society-wide and internationally relevant vision in his day. Bringing fresh vision to SRE and GRE in Australia has the potential to open a new society-strengthening chapter not only in NSW and Queensland where SRE and RI have the highest levels of coverage, but in all states and territories and beyond. In addition to the new Queensland peak bodies, since 1972 the NSW Christian churches' peak body ICCOREIS has been engaging with the NSW Department of Education on its SRE representative committee alongside other church and religions' representatives, including the new All Faiths SRE peak body, and key stakeholders within the department.

Gross and Rutland's research, while released in part in 2019,[51] has only just been released *in toto* and it is very early days to see how it will be engaged with by the various stakeholders in faith education in the Australian public education sector. But it is high time the Australian community, as those who pay for public education in the various jurisdictions, discovered what really happened in the 1830s and 1840s in eastern Australia to bring about the very focussed culture-shaping and society-building vision of Richard Bourke. That narrative has been obscured by secularist narratives read back into this period largely inspired by Marxist historiography, seeing Bourke's contribution as an exercise in establishing a dominant secularism. His vision and its results were nothing of the sort. They were deliberately nation-shaping through the Church Acts and the public education model specifically intended to overcome long-standing disenfranchisement of religious

---

[50] Ibid., 'Conclusion and Recommendations' including 'Implications for Future Research', pp. 267-74.
[51] Zehavit Gross and Suzanne D. Rutland: *How in-faith religious education strengthens social cohesion in multicultural Australia*, Storytelling and Visualisation by McCrindle.com.au, (booklet and visualisation sheet), Better Balanced Futures 2019.

minorities and so to build a non-sectarian culture expressing common Christian beliefs and practices at its core. It has given Australia a form of pluralism that both acknowledges the Christian origins of much of Australia's common cultural values,[52] as well as providing significant capacity for building the successful multicultural society constructed since the end of the second world war that Australia now enjoys.

Peter Robinson

© 2021 Peter Kenneth Bradley Robinson

Bibliography

Zehavit Gross and Suzanne D. Rutland: *Special Religious Education in Australia and its Value to Contemporary Society*, Springer 2021.

Zehavit Gross and Suzanne D. Rutland: *How in-faith religious education strengthens social cohesion in multicultural Australia*, Storytelling and Visualisation by McCrindle.com.au, (booklet and visualisation sheet), Better Balanced Futures 2019.

David Hastie: The Latest Installment in the Whig Interpretation of Australian Education History: Catherine Byrne's *JORH* Article 'Free, Complulsory and (not) Secular', *Journal of Religious History* 41:3 (September 2017) pp. 386-403.

Hazel King: Bourke, Sir Richard (1777-1855), *The Australian Dictionary of Biography*, MUP 1966 (also at http://adb.anu.edu.au/biography/bourke-sir-richard-1806).

The Hon. Michael Kirby, *Sentinels of Secularism*, Fort Street High School Annual Speech Day Address, Sydney Town Hall, 21 February 2020.

---

[52] Piggin and Linder op. cit., pp. 574-83.

Alan A. Langdon: Religious Education in the Public (Government) Schools of New South Wales: Part II: Special Religious Education. *Journal of Christian Education* 35(2) (1992) pp. 5-25.

R. A. Markus: *Saeculum: History and Society in the Theology of St. Augustine*, Cambridge University Press 1970.

Stuart Piggin and Robert Linder: *The Fountain of Public Prosperity*, Volume 1 of *Evangelicals in Australian History (1740-1914)* Monash University Publishing 2018.

Jennifer Ridden: The Forgotten History of the Protestant Crusade: Religious Liberalism in Ireland, *Journal of Religious History* 31:1 (March 2007) pp. 78-102.

David Stoneman: *The Church Act: the expansion of Christianity or the imposition of moral enlightenment?* PhD, University of New England 2011.

David Stoneman: Richard Bourke: For the Honour of God and the Good of Man, *Journal of Religious History* 38:3 (Sept 2014) pp. 341-355.

State Library of NSW Archive webpage: 'The Church Act 1836', http://www2.sl.nsw.gov.au/archive/discover_collections/history_nation/religion/places/act.html.

Max Waugh: *Forgotten Hero. Richard Bourke, Irish-born Governor of New South Wales 1831-1837*, Australian Scholarly Publishing, Melbourne 2005.

Ann Maree Whenman: *In Good Faith: A historical study of the provision of religious education for Catholic children not in Catholic Schools in New South Wales. The CCD Movement 1880-2000.* PhD Australian Catholic University 2011.

Robert Withycombe, *Bertie Boyce: Pioneer Clergyman, Social Reformer*, Morning Star Publishing, Reservoir Victoria 2018.

TRANSMITTING A UNIVERSITY TRADITION: EDMUND CAMPION AND JOHN HENRY NEWMAN

Karl Schmude

Edmund Campion and John Henry Newman can both stake a large claim to importance in the idea of a Catholic university, and more broadly in the world of higher education. Given the pervasive influence that universities exert on education at the primary and secondary levels, and on the broader culture, the contributions of Campion and Newman are of enduring value.

My aim is to explore the significance of Campion and Newman as foundational figures of Catholic higher education - and of a truly *higher* education. I liken them, in the sphere of the university, to the pivotal role played by Saints Peter and Paul in the historical development of the Church.

Campion and Newman lived three centuries apart – Campion in the 16th century, amid the religious and political turmoil of the English Reformation, and Newman in the 19th century, a period of great religious and intellectual controversy. I imagine each of them, characteristically, in a cell. Campion at first occupied the secret cell where he was found and captured, the special hiding place in English Catholic houses used by Campion and other priests, during this period of persecution, in the event of a sudden raid by the authorities; and finally, the prison cell to which he was consigned in the Tower of London – a cell understatedly known as the 'Little Ease' because of its cramped shape, which prevented its occupant from standing or lying comfortably. From these cells in Elizabethan England, Campion, still a relatively young man, radiated energy and inspiration – the energy of a scholar and lecturer, a man of learning, and the inspiration of an apostle and martyr, a man of faith. I imagine him in his pain – not only physical pain, having been tortured on the rack and now facing the horror of being hanged, drawn and quartered, but also the mental and emotional anguish of a priest desperate to shepherd his people in the midst of persecution.

John Henry Newman, too, I picture in a cell – in his case, a scholar's cell; composing tirelessly at his desk, producing so many memorable works. In these writings, particularly his private letters and diaries, I sense his pain as well – the pain of isolation, both religious and cultural, and of frustration of his talents, especially during the last half-century of his life as a Catholic. Newman lived to a formidable age – he was almost 90 when he died – by contrast with the relative youth of Campion at his martyrdom (he was only 41). In each case, the cell they inhabited was a symbol of their religious fidelity. It was a consecrated place in which they lived out their vocation of witness to the truth. We can, perhaps, see it as, in Campion's case, a consecration of the martyr's heart, and in Newman's, a consecration of the teacher's mind. In each case, I imagine them in their cells as they lived out their last days, and I wonder if they called to mind the mission they had fulfilled of exalting the truth in their time, and building the 'idea' of a university for our time. Indeed, all time, including those of us in the 21st century.

Campion and Newman were both born in London, but they were quintessentially men of Oxford. Each was the outstanding Oxford figure of his time. Campion was a man of precocious brilliance. Several years after leaving Oxford, he was described by Lord Cecil, an architect of the English Protestant Reformation, as 'one of the diamonds of England'.[1] He was appointed a Fellow of St John's College, Oxford, at the age of 17. He attracted a personal following, and exercised an intellectual influence, that was not rivalled for another three centuries – until John Henry Newman did the same, attending Trinity College, Oxford, as an undergraduate and becoming a Fellow of Oriel College at the age of 21. Newman called Oxford 'the most religious university in the world',[2] and the institution played a decisive part in forming the religious and intellectual sensibilities of Campion in the 16th century, and of Newman in the 19th century.

Speaking of the members of the Oxford Movement, Newman said that Catholics did not influence their conversion to Catholicism. 'Oxford,' he said, 'made us Catholics'.[3] Campion and Newman each delivered memorable sermons in the University Church of St Mary the Virgin in Oxford. Campion did so indirectly when his work of apologetics called *Ten Reasons* was secretly printed and left on the pews of the church, arousing the hostility of the authorities and causing a massive search for him – said to be the largest manhunt at that time in English history – which culminated in his capture and execution. Newman also spoke at the University Church – in person, and frequently, when he served as Vicar (1828-1843) during his Anglican years.

---

[1] Richard Simpson, *Edmund Campion: a biography* (London: John Hodges, 1896), p.20.
[2] C.S. Dessain, *John Henry Newman* (London: Nelson, 1966), p.6. Cf. the comment of Christopher Dawson, *The Spirit of the Oxford Movement* (London: Sheed & Ward, 1933), p.87: '[Newman] saw that the anti-modern character of Oxford, its unutilitarian beauty, fitted it to be the representative of religious ideals and spiritual values in an age of secularism and material progress.'
[3] Ian Ker, *John Henry Newman: a biography* (Oxford: Oxford University Press, 1988), p.493.

Both Campion and Newman loved Oxford. The Oxford experience shaped their philosophy of education, and their devotion to the university as an institution.[4] Each tried to establish a Catholic university in Ireland – but each was unsuccessful at the time. Campion sought to revive a university that had lapsed, a papal foundation of the 14th century, which was later to materialise as Trinity College, Dublin. Newman was deeply engaged in the founding of the Catholic University of Ireland; and while it, too, did not flourish in Newman's lifetime, it inspired the lectures which he delivered in Dublin, which formed the foundation of his famous work, *The Idea of a University*.

What was Newman's 'idea' of a university? It was at once a positive concept shaped and sharpened by negative forces. The positive content was the study of various subjects or branches of knowledge – commonly called the 'liberal arts' – so as to enlarge and cultivate the mind and produce an integrated understanding of knowledge and truth. In this Newman stressed the compatibility – even more, the necessary interdependence – of religion and learning, of faith and reason, of revelation and the imagination, as forming the unity and universality of truth.[5]

At the same time, Newman's concept of a liberal education – the education that befits a free man, and particularly a free lay man, since Newman had a deep desire to foster an educated laity[6] – is heightened by the defects and distortions of higher education, which have remained to our own time, and indeed intensified; especially the utilitarian view which

---

[4] Simpson, *Edmund Campion*, p.21, and *The Letters and Diaries of John Henry Newman*, ed. Charles Stephen Dessain et al. (Oxford: Clarendon, 1961-77), Vol.XXI, p.303.
[5] John Henry Newman, *Fifteen Sermons Preached Before the University of Oxford* (London: Longmans, Green & Co, 1900), Sermons X and XI, pp.176-221.
[6] *Letters and Diaries*, Vol.XXI, p.327, and John Henry Newman, *The Idea of a University*, ed. I.T. Ker (Oxford: Clarendon, 1976), p.392.

confuses education with vocational training, and the clerical attitude which mistakes a university for a seminary.⁷

Campion, too, had a deep sense of a liberal education. However, by comparison with Newman's vast output, only fragments of his writings survive to illustrate his outlook. After leaving Oxford, he spent time in Ireland. His writings of that period reflect his rich understanding of university culture, combining habits of mind and demeanour that constitute the ideal student.⁸ A discourse he wrote in Ireland, entitled *The Academic Man*, was described by the English Jesuit, C.C. Martindale, as anticipating Newman's *Idea of a University*.⁹ Campion stressed, for example, the blending of morals and manners with the cultivation of learning; the importance of piety and humility as well as healthy habits of study and recreation. In Ireland, he offered this advice to a student:

> ...[B]ury yourself in your books, complete your course... keep your mind on the stretch... strive for the prizes which you deserve...Only persevere, do not degenerate from what you are, nor suffer the keen eye of your mind to grow dark and rusty.¹⁰

In an oration he delivered in France – at the seminary of Douai – not long afterwards, Campion was even more explicit on what was required of a student. The ideal student must keep his mind subtle, his memory active, his voice resonant; he should cultivate his pronunciation; his recreations are to be painting, playing the lute and writing music; and he should be devoted to languages – Latin, Greek and his own tongue, in which he must compose verses and

---

⁷ Ker, *John Henry Newman*, pp.382-3.
⁸ Simpson, *Edmund Campion*, p.34.
⁹ C.C. Martindale SJ, *Blessed Edmund Campion* (London: Catholic Truth Society, 1964), p.3.
¹⁰ Simpson, *Edmund Campion*, p.33.

epigrams; by his 16th year, he must be able to produce Greek iambic verse![11]

When Campion later arrived in the city of Prague, after his ordination as a Jesuit and before his return to England and eventual martyrdom, he engaged largely in educational activities, teaching in the liberal arts – especially philosophy and rhetoric at a Jesuit school – as well as giving displays of oratory and writing and producing plays. To a decisive extent, Campion embodied the qualities that Newman would readily identify, three centuries later, with his 'idea of a university'. They both embody the Catholic – and quintessentially Christian - intellectual vocation, which consists of certain distinctive attributes: a devotion to truth, a synthesis of higher faith and natural reason, an attitude of spiritual sacrifice and fidelity, a zeal for souls and the winning of salvation, and a certain daring in challenging the status quo.

These qualities have registered an impact on our religious and educational culture, not least in the names of Campion and Newman being invoked by various institutions (tertiary colleges, university clubs and residential halls, and secondary schools). I am myself associated with such an institution in Sydney, a university-level Catholic Liberal Arts college, Campion College Australia. Our reason for adopting the name of Campion flowed from his universal status as a scholar, martyr and saint, but also from his local links with Australia. He has long served as the patron saint of lay Catholic adult education in Australia, beginning in the 1930s when the Campion Society was born, and occurring again in the 1970s when the Campion Fellowship arose – the name of that Fellowship being harvested, several years later in America, by the Fellowship of Catholic Scholars.

This spirit of intellectual vocation, and the qualities it embodies, are strikingly evident in both Campion and Newman. In his biography of Campion, Evelyn Waugh

---

[11] Ibid, pp.36-7.

describes the process by which the Elizabethan scholar and saint came to realize what God was asking of him – in his fidelity to the truth, and to God:

> *Only by slow stages was it revealed to Campion how complete was the sacrifice required of him. He had powerful friends and a brilliant reputation. Surely with these it must still be possible to make a career in the world, without doing violence to his religion? Surely it was not expected of him to give up all?*[12]

In the case of Newman, too, the process of realization was slow and yet unremitting. He was acutely conscious of the sacrifices, both personal and social, he made in becoming a Catholic, and he lamented the loss of old associations and the displacement of memories.[13] His last sermon as an Anglican was called 'The Parting of Friends'.[14] He felt few personal consolations or rewards in the years following his conversion to Catholicism; having to endure, on the one hand, grievous misunderstanding, and on the other, repeated neglect of his talents and his potential value to the Church.[15] In this, no doubt, he underwent a continuing torment, as was experienced in the following century by another priest-convert from Anglicanism, Ronald Knox, who, in the words of a recent reviewer, suffered 'a mild martyrdom'.[16] Even the pangs of intellectual confession were sharply felt: in writing the *Apologia pro Vita Sua* (1864), Newman reported being 'constantly in tears, and constantly crying out with distress'.[17]

---

[12] Evelyn Waugh, *Edmund Campion* (London: Longmans, Green & Co, 1935), p.33.
[13] Ker, *John Henry Newman*, p.293.
[14] John Henry Newman, *Sermons Bearing on Subjects of the Day* (London: Rivington, 1844), pp.447-64.
[15] Ker, *John Henry Newman*, pp.520, 561.
[16] Isabel Quigly, "Mild and Bitter," *Times Literary Supplement* (29 March 2002), p.36.
[17] *Letters and Diaries*, Vol.XXI, p.107.

Both Campion and Newman understood that the Catholic intellectual vocation involved suffering – especially suffering for the truth, and suffering for souls. One mark of this was the battle for truth – the various controversies in which Campion and Newman engaged. Campion showed his willingness and skill in the work of apologetics he produced, *Ten Reasons,* and in his *Brag,* the short but crucial manifesto he wrote of his purpose in returning to England; as well as, following his capture, in the verbal defence he offered, during his trial, of the Catholic mission which he and others undertook to England. Newman, for his part, revealed at an early date his taste as well as his talent for controversy. As his biographer Ian Ker observed, Newman had a strongly logical mind and great powers of irony and sarcasm, which were especially effective in his satirical writings.[18]

The involvement of Campion and Newman in controversy – in the great debates of their respective times – is of instructive interest in relation to their contrasting personalities. Campion was a strikingly attractive figure. At Oxford he gained a loyal following among students: they flocked to his lectures and even imitated his mannerisms and dress style. He was a man of gentle courtesy but not reserved, delighting in oratory and the theatre. His biographer Evelyn Waugh describes him as 'magnetic and inspiring'.[19] Across the centuries, he comes to us as a man of unmistakable flair. Newman appears as a different personality – reserved, even shy; lonely and highly sensitive, though also robust in the face of adversity; and, living as he did so much longer than Campion, much affected by the enfeeblement of age.

I have emphasized, in exploring the witness that Campion and Newman gave to the Catholic intellectual vocation, their readiness to suffer for the truth. But a further dimension of their vocation was a willingness to suffer for souls. These are organically linked, in imitation of Christ's own statement,

---

[18] Ker, *John Henry Newman*, pp.157, 168.
[19] Waugh, *Edmund Campion*, p.62.

that 'I am the Way, the Truth and the Life' (John 14:6); but they are also treated in *The Idea of a University*, where Newman argues that, while the direct end of a university is knowledge, the indirect effects are religious.[20]

In Campion's case, there is his heroic virtue as a priest, at first during his six years at Prague, where he not only served an academic role but was also preacher and confessor and provider of succour to those in prison and in hospital; and then on his return to England, where he faced the hazards of a hunted priest as he ministered to his persecuted flock. One incident in particular epitomizes his pastoral ardour – and that is, his forgiveness of the man, George Eliot, who betrayed him to the authorities. (One might discern shades of Pope John Paul II, forgiving Mehmet Ali Agca in his Rome prison cell, following his assassination attempt in 1981 in St Peter's Square.) George Eliot visited Campion in his prison cell and confessed that, after his Judas-like act, he feared for his life. Campion urged him to seek God's mercy and do penance for the sake of his salvation. He then offered to provide for Eliot's safety by recommending him to a Catholic duke in Germany. This overture did not have the desired effect – Eliot returned to spying for the Protestant authorities – but it did produce another benefit. Campion's gaoler was present at his meeting with Eliot and was so swayed by Campion's greatness of heart that he became a Catholic.

Newman, too, exhibited a readiness to suffer for souls. His conversion to Catholicism did not loosen his bonds of sympathy with his Anglican friends. He recalled with feeling the long years where they worshipped side-by-side, but acknowledged that his very outspokenness was due to his conviction that 'the Catholic Church is the one ark of salvation',[21] and due also to the love that he harboured for their souls. As a priest, he had a deep pastoral sense, which

---

[20] Ker, *John Henry Newman*, p.381.
[21] John Henry Newman, *Certain Difficulties felt by Anglicans in Catholic Teaching* (London: Longmans, Green & Co, 1918), Vol.1, p.4.

his fame and his final elevation to Cardinal did not impair. Those whom God 'singularly and specially loves, He pursued with His blows, sometimes on one and the same wound, till perhaps they are tempted to cry out for mercy'.[22] Newman, indeed, thought that the very act of belief is not only intellectual but also moral. It depends on 'a right state of heart' and 'is perfected, not by intellectual cultivation, but by obedience'. In short, Newman said, 'We *believe*, because we *love*'.[23]

An important factor in the zeal for souls exhibited by both Campion and Newman was their exposure to popular Catholic culture and ordinary Catholic people. As Campion wrestled at Oxford with his mind and conscience over his religious allegiance, it proved significant that he moved to Ireland. There he lived in the family home of a friend, and, as Evelyn Waugh notes, 'for the first and last time in his life, he tasted the happiness of a normal, cultured household'.[24] He experienced the integrated tribal life of the Irish people, and the dependable routines and rhythms of a deeply religious culture.

Newman was also exposed to this Irish culture, during the seven years of his endeavours to establish a Catholic university in Dublin. He felt an enduring gratitude to the Irish people for the kindness they had shown him over the years – from his first visit in 1851. But at an earlier stage, both before and after his conversion, he had visited Italy and Sicily. He was intensely impressed by the quality of popular faith – '*everywhere* [he observed] a simple certainty in believing which to a Protestant or Anglican is quite astonishing'.[25] Newman also understood the nature of popular faith which, while it was often intermingled with pagan traditions and carried superstitions requiring purification, was nonetheless

---

[22] Ker, *John Henry Newman*, pp.709-10.
[23] John Henry Newman, *Fifteen Sermons Preached before the University of Oxford* (London: Longmans,, Green & Co, 1900), pp.234,236,250.
[24] Waugh, *Edmund Campion*, p.34.
[25] *Letters and Diaries*, Vol.XII, p.24.

far preferable to scepticism. '[He] who believes a little, but encompasses that little with the inventions of men, is undeniably in a better condition than he who blots out from his mind both the human inventions, and that portion of truth which was concealed in them'.[26]

The culture of popular belief and practice is central to the contributions of Campion and Newman to the cause of a university education inspired by faith as well as reason. Each was engaged in disputes that seemed to be simply ecclesiastical and political; essentially, at the time, a conflict between Catholicism and Protestantism. Yet the conflicts were far more profound, involving tensions that were transcendental - even apocalyptic - presenting the character of a crisis, both spiritual and cultural, with which we are now far more familiar.

Campion and Newman recognized that new forces were menacing the Christian faith, and, by extension, its institutions such as the Catholic university. Like Thomas More before him, Campion saw the threat posed by the power of the State when it was enlisted in a way that damaged the unity of the Church, and allowed political and earthly allegiance to become synonymous with religious and transcendental faithfulness.

Newman, on the other hand, was acutely alive to the looming danger of secularism – a threat to the fundamental viability of religious belief in Western society, which was not only becoming irreligious but anti-Christian. As Christopher Dawson pointed out, 'Newman was the first Christian thinker in the English-speaking world who fully realised the nature of modern secularism and the enormous change which was already in the process of development, although a century had still to pass before it was to produce its full harvest of destruction'.[27]

---

[26] John Henry Newman, *The Arians of the Fourth Century* (London: Longmans, Green & Co, 1895), p.85.
[27] Christopher Dawson, "Newman and the Sword of the Spirit," *The Sword of the Spirit* (August 1945), p.1.

In a remarkable sermon which Newman preached in 1873, entitled 'The Infidelity of the Future', he foresaw the magnitude of the threat posed by a militant secularism. 'Christianity', he said, 'has never yet had experience of a world simply irreligious', and 'the trials which lie before us are such as would appal and make dizzy even such courageous hearts as St Athansius, St Gregory I, or St Gregory VII. And they would confess that, dark as the prospect of their own day was to them severally, ours has a darkness different in kind from any that has been before it'.[28] It was no longer possible to depend on the orthodox faith of Protestants, while Catholics in England were likely to be seen as 'the enemies' of 'civil liberty' and 'national progress', and to face discrimination, particularly since they were too prominent to be ignored, and yet too weak to defend themselves.[29]

Both Campion and Newman possessed a prophetic sense that remains sharply relevant to our own times – and to the future of a Catholic university in our society. Frank Sheed said that Campion was 'the first modern man in English history . . . He was of 20th century cast'.[30] Campion was sensitive to the problem of the State in relation to the Church, and above all when it came to the enforcement of false religion.

No doubt the people of the 16th century were feeling their way on the precise relationship between religious and political institutions, especially when they fell into conflict over the primacy of a citizen's loyalty. But it is arguable that Campion saw, with piercing clarity, the extent to which the State could subject the prerogatives of God to the power of Caesar, and produce, not only a politicised Church, but a

---

[28] John Henry Newman, *Catholic Sermons of Cardinal Newman* (London: Burns & Oates, 1957), pp.121, 123.
[29] Ker, *John Henry Newman*, p.676.
[30] F.J. Sheed, *Sidelights on the Catholic Revival* (London: Catholic Book Club, 1940), p.19.

sacralised State – a growing phenomenon of post-modern times.

Newman, too, grappled with the issue of a State Church, but he extended his gaze beyond that ecclesiastical and political level to the more pervasive problems of culture and faith itself. A politicised Church brings the power of the State into the very mind and heart of the Church, so that the State determines and dictates rather than simply supports religious faith as a social option - a reversal of right order which leads to a fatal confusion of sacred and secular loyalties. There are abundant examples of this confusion in present-day Western society, particularly in the sphere of law, whether it is the legislature or the court; but perhaps the most striking instance of a politicised Church is present-day Islam, which compounds religion and politics in a social order elevated – even consecrated, one might say - by the impulses of nationalism. The lack of distinction in Islam between Church and State, between God and Caesar - and between faith and reason - is a plain and unnerving threat to the complacent, yet tenacious, secularism of the contemporary West. I think the resurgence of Islam in the 21st century has given new relevance, and new urgency, to the deeper consequences of the 16th century English Reformation. If Islam poses a great threat to Christianity in the 21st century, as Communism did in the 20th century, we can appreciate even more powerfully the importance for our time of the prophetic insight of Edmund Campion and John Henry Newman. Campion might be seen as a precursor of Newman. If the State can determine religion, it can also determine irreligion. It can impose apostasy. A politicised Church, in which the temporal displaces the transcendental, paves the way for a secularist culture, in which time-bound loyalties are elevated to timeless, and totalitarian ideology becomes a substitute for transcendental faith.

These principles are of direct relevance to the university, and specifically the Catholic university or any institution of learning informed by principles of faith as well as reason.

The university cannot finally maintain its integrity, its essential mission, as an educational institution, if it is at first politicised, and then secularized. As Christopher Dawson noted, in a secularist culture the Christian Churches cannot afford to be concerned only with their own institutions, especially schools. They must attend to secular institutions of learning as well.[31] Dawson focused on the Catholic Church in particular, but his insights also relate to other Christian communities and their institutions. In reflecting on the idea of a Catholic university in the 21st century, we must also address the idea of a *university*.

I have described Campion and Newman as the Peter and Paul of Catholic higher education. I hope this is not an unduly excessive comparison, but, in pondering the importance of Campion and Newman, both for their own time and for ours, I have been struck by certain parallels with the lives and contributions of St Peter and St Paul.

In their sense of intellectual vocation, Campion and Newman may be seen to resemble St Paul – in their facility with ideas and with language, their deep convictions founded in faith as well as reason, and their devotion to learning. St Paul was a convert, as was Campion and Newman; and, just as he provided a theological foundation and an intellectual architecture for the Christian faith, so Campion and Newman supplied the intellectual underpinning for the Christian university.

In certain other ways, Campion and Newman resemble St Paul – in their preaching and power of oratory; and in their daring, a brave eagerness to take on the prevailing intellectual order and challenge it with the Truth of Christ. To this might be added Campion's personal prowess – a physical daring, an undeniable verve, manifested by St Paul in his perilous journeys, and by Campion in his period of constantly evading the English authorities, until, like St Paul, he was captured and martyred.

---

[31] Christopher Dawson, *The Crisis of Western Education* (London: Sheed & Ward, 1961), p.112.

Newman, too, displayed Pauline qualities. For one thing, Newman and St Paul were great letter writers. For another, they both sought to adapt the Church to new conditions – Newman's grasp of secularism helping to prepare the Church for a different culture, mirroring St Paul's role in developing the Church beyond its cradle in Judaism to meet the different circumstances of a Gentile world. Newman had a special respect for St Paul because of his humanity – 'his intimate sympathy and compassionateness for the whole world, not only in its strength, but in its weakness; in the lively regard with which he views everything that comes before him, taken in the concrete'.[32]

Campion and Newman resemble St Peter in the unmistakable qualities of leadership which each displayed. They embodied and projected a vision of learning, of the intellectual apostolate, of the university, that bears respectful comparison with the broader leadership in the Church exercised by St Peter. They also showed a capacity for organizational development, one of the qualities of a leader, as revealed in their respective desire to found universities in Ireland.

And yet the educational vision of Campion and Newman was based on the university as the culmination of formal education, which relied on the preparatory importance of earlier education. Campion, as a young schoolboy in London, exemplified this education by giving the speech of welcome to the visiting Queen Mary on the occasion of her visit in 1553 to his London school. Later in Prague, he enacted the tradition of classical teaching that marked the fundamental vocation of the Jesuit Order from its beginnings. Three centuries later, Newman established the Oratory School in Birmingham – and subsequently inspired other educational initiatives, at both the secondary and tertiary levels.

---

[32] Ker, *John Henry Newman*, p.484.

Their ideas, and the institutions they have influenced, are not simply of interest to past generations. They continue to be of creative importance. They offer ways of responding to the educational challenges of our time – and provide inexhaustible sources of inspiration.[33]

---

[33] This chapter has been presented in earlier forms – first, as a paper, 'Campion and Newman: the Peter and Paul of Catholic Higher Education', at a conference of the Fellowship of Catholic Scholars, 'The Idea of the Catholic University for the 21st Century,' 28 September 2007, in Washington DC, and in a revised form at a conference of the Australian Chesterton Society, 'A Third Spring: G.K. Chesterton and the Convert Cardinals,' at Campion College, 31 October 2015. It was published in *Quadrant* in May 2016 under the title, 'Campion, Newman and the Intellectual Apostolate'.

FR PAUL STENHOUSE'S WRITINGS: A PERSISTENT PEDAGOGY CONFRONTING THE GRAMSCIAN RESET

Wanda Skowronska

Many have remembered Father Paul Stenhouse (1935-2019) as a scholar, editor, writer, publisher and priest. Also very notable is his extraordinary pedagogical role from the 1960s onwards. While many were bopping with insouciance to the Beatles, the Easy beats, Little Patti and Col Joy, with academics calling for the Parisian barricades, revolution, and deconstructionism, Fr Stenhouse formed a powerful resistance in his writings to the growing anti-Christian and anti-rational animus.

His strategic gifts were particularly evident in that remarkable, doughty phenomenon- the longest lasting journal in Australia's history – *Annals*. Here he especially showed that his writing had a pedagogical purpose aiming at the scholar, religious, layman and student writing on many subjects but always preserving our identity and culture. As his friend Karl Schmude observed perceptively of his writings in *Annals*:

> *[He] blended to a marked degree the "high" and the "low" traditions of religion and culture. He was immersed in the tradition of intellectual*

probing and aesthetic appreciation – in philosophy and theology, art and architecture, literature and music ... He knew that the life of intellectual penetration needed to strengthen and validate the spiritual intuitions and habits of ordinary people, and he would publish excerpts from early and later authors – from the Church Fathers to John Henry Newman and G.K. Chesterton – who fused these traditions of insight and experience in illuminating ways.[1]

In 1964, he became business manager for *Annals*, shortly after his ordination in 1963. Whether he realised it or not in 1966 when he took over full editorship – his use of short essay was a brilliant communication tactic – with acute, succinct, often provocative doses of reality - in a century where as T.S. Eliot had observed humankind 'cannot bear too much reality.' In this way he was an early strategist, waging guerrilla war against cultural amnesia. The *Little Blue Book*, as the *Annals* was called, had always punched above its weight from its beginnings in 1889. It had affirmed Catholic identity, with stories of missionaries, church news, history and theology, sent to city folk and isolated bush communities. It continued to do so when Fr Stenhouse confronted the post-modernist deluge. And it lasted. In a 1989 centenary overview, Fr Stenhouse pointed to its success, asking:

> How many today have even heard of *The Boomerang*, *The Illustrated Sydney News*, *The Picturesque Atlas of Australasia*, the *Australian Standard*, the *Lone Hand*, the *Stockwhip and Satirist*, the *Express*, the *Melbourne Star* or *the Sydney Evening News*? [2]

---

[1] Karl Schmude, "Fr Paul Stenhouse MSC (1935-2019) – Catholic Editor Extraordinaire", Catholic Herald, 11 December 2019. https://catholicherald. co.uk/fr-paul-stenhouse-msc-1935-2019-catholic-editor-extraordinaire-2/

[2] Paul Stenhouse's earlier memoir of Annals is entitled: "The Annals of *The Annals:* 'Within a Shining Pool'", The *Australasian Catholic Record*, July 1994, 273. Much factual material about Annals can be obtained from this source.

Early on (from 1967 to 1976) the *Annals*, then called *Annals Australia*, featured what were called *Catechetical Supplements* every month for teachers and students, eight pages of quotations, questions, photos, illustrations, alongside comments on contemporary, social, and religious issues. No single article exceeded a page, most were a half column, and there were photos with comment. For example, a 1968 edition deals with the issues of friendship, loneliness, and drugs. Advice, practical and spiritual, was given as to what to do if lonely, questions about drug taking – with critiques of sham answers, given by current drug takers such as like Timothy Leary with and Beatle Paul McCartney who said: 'If the politicians would take LSD there wouldn't be any more war or poverty or famine.'[3]

In the same edition there was also a comment by Lord Ritchie Calder: 'Psychotropic agents! The tranquilliser in one pocket: the 'pep' pill in the other. Drugs to dispel nightmares, rugs to invoke dreams…this is caricature of one type of modern man.' (*Annals*, March,1968, *Catechetical Supplement*, I). And then came Malcolm Muggeridge's view: 'Whatever life is, or is not about, it's not we may be sure to be expressed in terms of drug stupefaction … or psychedelic fantasies.'[4] There were also quotations from younger people against drug-taking, for example from Midget Farrelly, and a challenge to Albert Camus' view that life is absurd. A lot is packed into one educational supplement!

Fr Stenhouse engaged a team – brothers, nuns, various educators – whose supervised the content of the *Supplements*. Of this, his long-time friend, MSC priest, Fr Peter Malone, states:

> He [Fr Stenhouse] went to North Sydney, met a Josephite sister called Sister Peter and she opened up the whole world of religious

---

[3] *Annals*, March,1968, *Catechetical Supplement*, i.
[4] Malcolm Muggeridge, in "Four recent case histories", *Annals*, Catechetical Supplement, March 1968, p.iii.

education to him. He got inspired then to have catechetical supplements in the Annals on all the topics of the time that were important, especially for secondary school students ... it was quite extraordinary ...[5]

The supplements covered many issues: the search for meaning, the changing church, relationships, war, racism, capital punishment and abortion. As regards the latter issue, *Annals* got publicly attacked for its trouble but did not resile from presenting the Catholic perspective.

Fr Stenhouse himself recalls that the period 1968 – 1974, 'was one of phenomenal success for *Annals*', adding, 'it wasn't all plain sailing as anyone growing up at that time will remember.'[6] He recalled that *Annals* was bought by Catholic, non-Catholic and State schools! He recalled that Chaplains in non-Catholic schools welcomed the religious education material which was 'thoroughly Australian in content and design' with an unashamedly Christian framework. [7] *Annals'* circulation climbed from 25,000 in 1960s to 58,000 in 1972. Some months 70,000 copies sold. The supplements included references for teachers on the Church Fathers and documents ... nothing was haphazard. At the beginning of the year teachers and priests were notified of the course that *Annals* was planning.

Some may ask how Fr Stenhouse handled the burning issue of the Vietnam War? Fr Stenhouse had such equanimity that he could speak to opposing sides of an issue with equal success. While offering counsel and support to Vietnam war protestors, he also offered counsel to those who supported the war, saying in a 1966 *Annals* editorial, '[l]et us pray for peace, work for peace, but let us also assess

---

[5] A Reflection by Father Peter Malone MSC: Service Before the Interment Of Father Paul Stenhouse MSC Saint Mary's Towers, Douglas Park, 2:30 PM, Wednesday, 27th November 2019. From author's copy of the text.
[6] Ibid.
[7] Ibid.

realistically the enemy's tactics and prepare our deterrence accordingly.'⁸

Annals was also a pedagogical influence in theatre and film, a role it never lost up to its last edition, where Catholics looked to its reviews as a guide. In earlier years, Fr Stenhouse was a friend of Bill Collins and watched films at Collins' home cinema). *Annals* reviewer Trish Kavanagh, (a cousin of Fr Stenhouse) wondered why she got allocated the best seats in the house in theatres. A staff member informed her that if a play or film got a good review in *Annals,* then it was guaranteed large audience. So, it was wise to treat *Annals* reviewers with great respect!

As the 1970s progressed, the rising feminist, anti-colonial and Marxist ideologies seeped into universities and the wider culture, later solidifying into what we saw in the 1980s and beyond. Christopher Dawson had seen and lamented this in his 1950s work *Religion and the Rise of Western Culture*, saying:

> ... *the vital subject of the creative interaction of religion and culture in the life of Western society has been left out and almost forgotten, since from its nature it has no place in the organized scheme of specialized disciplines. It has been left to the amateur and to the man of letters. It is only thanks to some exceptional foundation like that of the Gifford Lectures that it is possible to find an opportunity to bring it into relation with academic studies.*⁹

As Dawson did with the Gifford lectures, Fr Stenhouse did with *Annals*. However, as the demand for the educational supplements waned in the later 70s, Fr Stenhouse perceived the deeper need to educate the wider public, to penetrate the cultural fog. He put focus on Biblical facts, the Church Fathers, ancient and modern history, reasoned explanations for church teachings, religion, architecture, and the rise of

---

⁸ Paul Stenhouse, Editorial, *Annals*, September 1966.
⁹ Dawson, *Religion and the Rise of Western Culture* (NY: Doubleday, 1950), 13.

culture, especially going to the sources. He did this with a pithy, pedagogical, and moral force.

For example, in a 1983 *Annals* editorial about euthanasia, Fr Stenhouse describes Louis Pasteur's paralysis at age 46, how Pasteur reflected on the richness of these years, where he not only went to do his most brilliant work, when incapacitated, amazing even himself, and appreciating the value of his very restricted life. After telling similar stories, Fr Stenhouse quietly adds that a certain Fritz Sawade, in Kiel in 1959, was arrested and identified as Professor Werner Heyde, the Nazi Obersturmbannführer who was responsible for killing hundreds of thousands of unwanted human beings and for refining the techniques of extermination during the war.[10] Fr Stenhouse had made his point.

Sometimes Fr Stenhouse's pedagogical counterattack was directed at countering misinformation on Catholicism. It was very unwise to present inaccurate information to Fr Stenhouse on Biblical sources. He often took a deep breath before a polite but irrefutable fusillade of facts reduced listeners to silence.

As Stuart Rowland, accomplished member of the Melbourne Bar, stated of Fr Stenhouse:

> *He was very tolerant in allowing one to express opinions but this laser accuracy would home in on the facts and assumptions that underpinned those opinions: he would have made a devastating advocate had he chosen the law.*[11]

His series of articles on answering 'Bible Christians', written between 1986 and 1988 had an overt pedagogical

---

[10] Paul Stenhouse, "Consequences of Euthanasia - Voluntary and Compulsory", *Annals Australasia*, Editorial, October 1983.
https://web.archive.org/web/20150907135335/http://jloughnan.tripod.com/pasteureuth.htm
[11] Taken from a personal account of Stuart Rowland, sent to the author.

purpose demonstrating this 'laser accuracy', exposing various distortions about the Catholic faith and pointing out that none of them is novel. These articles were later put together in a publication entitled *Catholic Answers to 'Bible' Christians: A Light on Biblical Fundamentalism* (1988 in two volumes, still sold from the *Annals* office) underwent many reprintings.[12]

For example. he took on the myth that the Protestants made the Bible available and that there was no Bible in English before Wycliffe (1382) – a notion asserted by American Protestant Bible Teacher and anti-Catholic polemicist Loraine Boettner. Fr Stenhouse tears apart Boettner's case, piece by piece, replying that: the whole Bible was translated into Saxon by the Venerable Bede (672-735); King Alfred (848-899) translated parts of Exodus and the Acts of the Apostles; that King Alfred exhorted his readers to "be busily occupied in reading Sacred Scripture and in frequent prayer"; Pope Agatho, in a Council in Rome in 679 AD strongly encouraged sacred reading by all, referring to the words of Holy Scripture; the Council of Cloveshoe (of Clyff) insisted on the reading of Sacred Scripture by everyone.[13] In reply to the notion that Bibles were chained to pulpits or walls to prevent the faithful accessing them, he says that it took at least 10 months to write out the Bible's 35,877 verses on 6,391 pages, so the reason it was chained a public place was quite the opposite - to make it available to all, as with any library.[14]

Fr Stenhouse then used his well-known tactic – using words of Protestants to support the Catholic case. He quotes Protestant Rev. S.R. Maitland, librarian to the Archbishop of Canterbury, who in 1844 demolished forever the myth that

---

[12] Paul Stenhouse MSC, Ph.D. "*Catholic Answers to 'Bible' Christians: A Light on Biblical Fundamentalism*" (Sydney: Chevalier Press, 1988), 1. Further references to this issue are taken from this book, available from the *Annals* office.
[13] Ibid., 1
[14] Ibid., vii ff

'No Catholic (in pre-reformation England) ever knew his Bible well.'[15] Maitland states that St Aldhelm sailed into Dover Harbour in 715 AD with a Bible, and presented it to the people of Malmesbury; and refers to Offa, King of the Mercians who presented a Bible to the Church at Worcester in 780AD. Maitland adds there was not a single instance in which the Bible was kept from the people.[16]

Just to put a few more nails in the coffin, Fr Stenhouse cites the fact that there were no fewer than nine Catholic editions of the Bible in German before 1483, the year Luther was born! Calvinist David Clement documented his seeing two copies of a Catholic version of the Bible, made in 1466 and kept in the Senatorial Library in Leipzig, pointing out that at least sixteen editions of this translation were made before 1552 - one at Strasbourg, five at Nuremberg and ten at Augsburg. He presents a mass of evidence to prove that pre-Reformation editions of the Bible in the vernacular were found in Italy, Spain, the Low Countries, Poland, Sweden, Iceland, older Arabic, Syriac, Ethiopian, Armenian, not to mention the Chinese and Indian translations being produced in Rome *at the same time* Luther was working on his translation/version of the Bible.

As some may know, Fr Stenhouse temporarily left the *Annals* in 1976 when he was invited to be the Private Secretary to the MSC Father General (later Auxiliary Bishop) Eugene Cuskelly (1924 - 1999) in Rome. This period was to deepen and enrich his future writing. Becoming an 'expert' on Roman history – he gave friends memorable and fascinating tours of Catholic Rome. Then he went to Dubrovnik (Croatia), to complete his PhD thesis entitled: 'A Critical Edition of the Kitab al-Tarikh of Abu'l-Fath.' (Abu'l-Fath was a Samaritan priest and the Kitab al-Tarikh was the title of one of his works). Who would have thought Communist Yugoslavia was the ideal place to write a thesis? And yet it was.

---

[15] Ibid., 2.
[16] Ibid., 2

According to fellow MSC Fr Michael Fallon, it took some time to find an examiner for his three-volume PhD thesis, for Fr Stenhouse was the only person in the world at that stage who understood its content. He provided dictionaries so that the examiners could read it. In time, his contribution was a pedagogical gift to scholars, and the University of Sydney Mandelbaum site entry says of his work:

> *Based on an analysis of all the important MSS and accompanied by copious notes on the Arabic original, this work is the first translation of the whole of this most important of the Samaritan chronicles into English.*[17]

After his doctoral studies, Fr Stenhouse took on the reins of *Annals* again in the early 1980s providing an even deeper historical, linguistic, and richer Biblical understandings in the post-modernist miasma. He also taught at Sydney University and marked HSC papers in Hebrew – complaining to the Board of Studies that the standard of Hebrew had gone down.

He enlisted many writers from different fields in his pedagogical counter-attack to post-modernism - James Waldersee, Giles Auty, Jude Dougherty, Michael O'Connor and in the words Professor Marek Chodakiewicz's, '[h]e made the *Annals* a powerhouse of Catholic intellectual prowess.'[18] With this knowledge, he took readers on remarkable journeys of Biblical significance to Jerusalem, Petra and Damascus and infused *Annals* with stories of the suffering Catholics in Kashmir, Syria, Uzbekistan, Lebanon,

---

[17] Entry in Mandelbaum Publishing appears on its website as follows.
'Father Dr Paul Stenhouse: Mandelbaum Studies in Judaica 1 The Kitab al Tarikh of Abu'l-Fath: The Chronicle of Abu'l-Fath'.
https://learning.mandelbaum.usyd.edu.au/mandelbaum-publishing/father-dr-paul-stenhouse/
[18] Marek Jan Chodakiewicz, "Fr Paul Stenhouse, R.I.P., *Crisis Magazine*, January 21. https://www.crisismagazine.com/2020/fr-paul-stenhouse-r-i-p

Papua New Guinea, East Timor, Africa, Kashmir and Albania and Armenia. not to mention the fate of East European countries. The reader could feel he or she was an Indiana Jones, travelling with Fr Stenhouse along lesser known, historically fascinating pathways.

For example, where otherwise would you have understood the problems of the Armenian Christians in Nagorno Karabakh and the ongoing Islamic-Christian conflict there? Through the efforts of Armenian priest (later bishop) Anton Totonjian, Fr Stenhouse organised journeys to Armenia in 1991and 1995 with photographer Jacob Majarian and saw it all, speaking to refugees in Nagorno Karabakh.[19] He also saw that the 'end' of the Soviet Union did not bring an end to food shortages and pervasive military control. Boarding an Aeroflot flight, Jacob and Fr Stenhouse observed water falling from the plane's ceiling and saw a passenger drink an entire bottle of vodka on the flight to Yerevan. Anyone who has flown Aeroflot would understand.

It was because of such intrepid flights that Fr Stenhouse told us about the '11th century monastery of Yeritsmankants, in the Mardakert region of Northeastern Nagorno Karabagh' with the pedagogical note:

Karabagh was cut off from Armenia and ceded to Azerbaijan by Stalin, and the territory is now claimed back by Armenia. Armenia was the first nation state to embrace Christianity when Gregory the Illuminator carried the Faith there in 301 A.D. Before he set off on this journey Gregory visited Rome and received the blessing of Pope Marcellinus [296-304] the 28th successor of St Peter and a predecessor

---

[19] The details of this journey and Jacob's friendship with Father Stenhouse are taken from a written account of a meeting with Jacob on 19 March 2020. Fr Stenhouse's friend, Father Tontonjian, wrote about the situation of the Armenians in Australia available on the online *Annals Archive*:
https://web.archive.org/web/20150907123141/http://jloughnan.tripod.com/armenschool.htm. Fr Anton Tontonjian, "First School for Armenian Catholics in Australia", *Annals Australia*, November/December 1984.

of Pope John Paul II, the 263rd successor of St Peter, whose love for Armenia and the Armenians is well-known.[20]

No teacher could have given a more succinct lesson in 6 lines!

Fr Stenhouse had friends in many communities. Among his friends were members of the Lebanese, Trinidadian, Tobagan, Indonesian, Vietnamese and Malaysian communities. There was also Henryk Skrzynski, Polish survivor of Auschwitz, who made a vow to God if he survived the war, he would write a book about the Jewish milieu of the Virgin Mary. He survived and wrote *The Jewess Mary* after meeting Fr Stenhouse who published it via Chevalier Press.

Another long-time friend Phillip Collignon, then director of Aid to the Church in Need, recalled that in the Ukraine on 30 March 30, 1991, he and Fr Stenhouse witnessed the return of the head of the Byzantine Rite Catholics, free for the first time since 1945. He writes:

> *Myroslav Ivan Lubachivskyj was coming home after 52 years. He is the first Catholic Metropolitan Archbishop of Galicia to set foot in Lviv since April 11, 1945, when Metropolitan (later Cardinal) Josef Slipj was imprisoned, along with the entire Episcopate, 1735 priests, 1090 nuns and tens of thousands of lay Catholics. All the Ukrainian Byzantine Catholic bishops died in prison except Josef Slipj who paid for his refusal to convert to Russian Orthodoxy with a further seven years in prison and exile to Siberia. He was freed only in 1963 after the intervention of Pope John XXIII.*[21]

---

[20] Caption to the front and back cover photos of the *Annals* article entitled "he 11th century monastery of Yeritsmankants, in the Mardakert region of Northeastern Nagorno Karabagh," June 2003. https://web.archive.org/web/20150907113551/http://jloughnan.tripod.com/armenpics.htm

[21] Paul Stenhouse, CHRIST IS TRULY RISEN: *The return of Great Archbishop Cardinal Myroslav Lubachivskyj to his faithful Byzantine-Rite Catholics*, Easter 1991, *Annals Australasia*, May 1991.

Again superb succinct, pedagogical reportage!

Of course, the work of Fr Stenhouse cannot be understood without his understanding of the Middle East. He wrote about Lebanon, Syria and Israel. Hebrew other historians and linguists to write for him on this subject, publishing some of their articles in *Annals,* among them those of Samir Khalil Samir SJ, John Pontifex, Walter Brandmüller, Robert Spencer, Andrew Bostom, Nina Shea, Professor Jude Dougherty and John Newton. He had friends with first-hand experience of Islamic societies, such as Ganesh Sahathevan and his Lebanese friend Joseph Assaf.

During the Lebanese war he described his travels to Lebanon in a hand-written 1987 diary found in his office.[22] Travelling by car with two Maronite monks, he notes several Lebanese and Syrian checkpoints along the way:

> *There were at least 15 Syrian army checkpoints through which we had to pass before arriving at Zahle. The trip was saddening as many homes along the roadside were in ruins and if their occupants had been inside when the shells struck, they would have been killed ... We passed a church that was being used as a weapons store by the Syrians ... we also noticed two or three Syrian soldiers wearing crosses, one of them was a Maronite.*[23]

In Beirut he notes laconically that 'despite the problem of snipers, I took photos of West Beirut.'[24]

---

https://web.archive.org/web/20150907152852/http://jloughnan.tripod.com/ukraineb.htm

[22] The original hand-written diary, a small black notebook, was on Fr Stenhouse's desk in the office of Fr Stenhouse at the Monastery of the Sacred Heart in Kensington, Sydney. It did not have page numbers. I express gratitude to Fr Chris McPhee for permission see Fr Stenhouse's general papers early in 2020; also, to Peter Macinante for locating the passport of Fr Stenhouse which matched his travel dates, 16-24 April, to the diary dates.
[23] Ibid.
[24] Ibid.

During the Lebanese War (1975-1990), he wanted to get medication to Lebanese and Syrian refugees. This was extremely difficult as the normal means of sending anything by post or courier were unlikely to succeed. In 1987, during the Lebanese war, Fr Stenhouse asked (begged) for medications from pharmaceutical companies in Australia and himself took his large consignment of donated medicines to Cyprus. From there he hired a boat and crew, headed for Lebanon, and sailed into a Lebanese port, and was thus able to get the medications to where they were needed.[25] Of this Professor Marek Chodakiewicz remarked:

> *Unauthorized and unorthodox, the mission was a success and a prime example of what the Missionaries of the Sacred Heart could accomplish. Before this audacious stunt, virtually all aid moving through the so-called proper channels had fallen into the hands of thugs and militias. Our priest figured out a way to outsmart them as well as the dead hand of international bureaucracy.*[26]

On Islamic matters, Fr Stenhouse managed to pitch his writing to both layman and academic. He points out that Islam's sacred book, the Qur'an (or Koran), claims to be the first book written in Arabic known to scholars, allegedly being the direct word of Allah given to Muhammad by Allah himself, through an angel from 612 to 632 AD. In a 1989 *Annals* article he outlines as a teacher would, that the teachings in this Islamic text are 'in the form of 114 Suras or chapters made up ... of 6,200 verses (the most ancient text of the Koran dates from 776 AD).'[27] In his explanatory style,

---

[25] This was related by Father Stenhouse to several friends, among them Malaysian friend Chris Lim, who related it to me.

[26] Marek Jan Chodakiewicz, "Fr Paul Stenhouse, R.I.P.", *Crisis Magazine*, 21 January. https://www.crisismagazine.com/2020/fr-paul-stenhouse-r-i-p

[27] Paul Stenhouse, "Islamic Law: questions no one will ask", *Annals Australia*, October, 1989. https://web.archive.org/web/20150907195957/http://jloughnan.tripod.com/islaw.htm

he points out that Islamic teachings are not restricted to the Qur'an but include:

> *The Sunna or 'conduit' containing what are variously estimated to be from 100,000 to 750,000 Hadith of 'sayings' of the prophet dating from around 855 AD ...*

Like a good teacher, explains clearly that there are four basic pillars of Islam – the Qur'an, the Sunna, the Ijma (or consent of the Mujtahidun or learned men), and the Kiyas (legal prescriptions from the Koran and the Sunna).[28] Again, so much explained within a few paragraphs.

He was always good at exploding myths. While Gramscian critiques of Western Christianity were praising Marxism in educational institutions, Fr Stenhouse's published articles by ex-Communist writer Rupert Lockwood, outlining Marxist horrors. Imagine this - a former writer for *Pravda* wrote for *Annals* in the 1990s! Fr Stenhouse and Lockwood understood clearly that perpetual anti-western critique permeating humanities departments from the 1970s onwards aimed at destroying what Gramsci called the west's 'cultural superstructure' - religion, marriage, notions of democracy and individualism. As Herbert Marcuse often declared, in works such as *Eros and Civilisation* (1953) and *One Dimensional Man* (1964,) the west did not need to be transformed, it had to be eliminated.

Fr Stenhouse, in a 2003 *Annals* article entitled 'Cambridge Spies and Marxism's Post-Modernist Front', gives a forensic analysis of post-modernism's attempts to erase the culture of the west. He highlights the Cambridge spies who in the inter-war years, turned against their own country and became Soviet agents, seeing in Marxism a utopian future which would eliminate the Judeo-Christian past. They

---

Fr Stenhouse used the spelling 'Koran' more in his early work and more widely used 'Qur'an' in his later writings.
[28] Ibid.

certainly wished to 'cancel' their culture.[29] Fr Stenhouse quotes from Michael Straight, who almost joined the 'Cambridge apostles', but who got out in time:

> *We were among the last of the Utopians ... we repudiated all versions of original sin ... we were not aware that civilization was a thin and precarious trust ... only maintained by rules and conventions skilfully put across and guilefully preserved. We had no respect for traditional wisdom and the restraints of custom. We lacked reverence ...*[30]

In 2003, Fr Stenhouse noted their influence in the current loathing for western culture:

> *New recruits for a hypothetical 21st century post-modernist university dining-club at a university near you, would be bombarded with scepticism about the past and the present. 'The truth is unknowable and beyond the reach of us all,' they will be told. 'Historical research is impossible because history is "fiction".' The difference between historical "fact" and "falsehood" is ideological.' As we can't know anything about the past, it's better to ignore it; or to dismiss it as ideologically distorted by those who recorded it.*[31]

Fr Stenhouse was alert to the past century's illusions, ideologies, woke thinking, and the post 1989 anti-spiritual animus. He left a legacy of extraordinary and powerful pedagogy in his unique brand of myth-busting suffused with equanimity. One could quote many verses of Scripture here - perhaps the ones that resonate are those of Ecclesiastes:

---

[29] Fr Paul Stenhouse, "Cambridge Spies and Post-modernist lies," *Annals Australasia,*" March 2003.
The best known of these spies are Kim Philby, Douglas Maclean, Guy Burgess, Anthony Blunt and John Cairncross. They all rose to high positions in English society and passed valuable information to the Soviets which resulted in the deaths of many western intelligence officers.
[30] Fr Stenhouse quotes copiously from: Michael Straight, *After Long Silence* (UK: Norton, 1983).
[31] Fr Paul Stenhouse, "Cambridge Spies and Post-modernist lies."

'the quiet words of the wise are more to be heeded than the shouting of a ruler.' (Ecc 9: 17).

May Fr Stenhouse's wisdom and teaching be, studied, learned from, and honoured for evermore.

SEEKING THE RIGHT BALANCE OF FAMILY, CHURCH AND SCHOOL FOR PASSING ON THE FAITH

Ben and Julianna Smith

Introduction

In this talk I wish to look closely at the way in which the institutions of the family, the parish/Church and the school interact to influence how faith is passed on to the next generation.

This talk will be composed of three parts. Firstly, it will briefly examine how these three institutions have worked together in the past and in the present. I will then review some recent thinking on this issue to provide a guide to future approaches. In the second part, I will share my family's experience of how the family, the Church and the school have worked together in four different situations. In the final part of the talk, I will bring the first two sections of a talk into conversation to explore some ideas for how these institutions can collaborate to create the best synergy for passing on the faith.

Part 1

Since the advent of universal education in the late 19th century, the Catholic Bishops of Australia turned to religious teaching orders, that largely originating from Ireland or France, to help staff the development of a Catholic school system. The Catholic school system gave Catholic parents an option for educating their children in matters spiritual and temporal that were separate from State and other denominational schools. At that point in time, Catholics parents had a relatively low level of educational attainment. The general attitude of Catholic parents was that they *entrusted* the bulk of the educational task to Catholic schools. Furthermore, Catholic parishes acted as a hub of social activity. Initiatives such as the Catholic Youth Organisation and other apostolates provided sporting, and cultural avenues to occupy young adults and build friendships that often blossomed into marriages. New Catholic families formed and the cycle was repeated.

Up until the time of Vatican II that was held from 1962-65, Catholics largely lived in a parallel universe from the surrounding society that was mediated by their connections to school and parish. From around 1965, key elements of this culture started to breakdown.

In the late 1960's and 70s there was a significant exodus of people from the priesthood and religious life. Combined with this exodus, there was a collapse in new vocations to the priesthood and religious life. Consequently, there was a growing proportion of lay teachers in Catholic schools and the Catholic identity of the schools was impacted by the reduced witness of consecrated religious. Furthermore, parish attendance dropped and a growing gap emerged between the parish community and the school community. The school effectively became the faith community for many Catholic and their preference was for a more culturally acceptable version of Catholicism.

The shift that started in the mid 1960's has impacted a few generations of Catholics and research has found a number of indicators of reducing faith practice. A leading researcher of Catholic schools, Br Marcellin Flynn found almost 20 years ago that:

...among the graduates of our Catholic schools, between 92 and 98 per cent of young adults do not practice their faith in the usually understood ways, or engage the life of the Church in any regular manner.[1]

In the context of Tasmania, whose Catholic population has historically been around 30% smaller compared to other states, the percentage of non-Catholics being educated in Catholic schools has gradually increased from 46% in 2008[2] to 58% in 2018[3].

I am proud to say that significant efforts are being made in Tasmanian Catholic schools to respond to the challenges that have emerged over recent decades. The implementation of the Archbishop's Charter for Catholic schools is proceeding well but it will take a number of years to fully take effect.

Beyond Entrustment

The current environment is extremely challenging for a Catholic family that are attempting to take seriously the duty to instruct their children in the faith. The entrustment model of previous generations has reached a crisis point and some

---

[1] http://www.rec.bne.catholic.edu.au/Pages/Theological-Background-Details.aspx?tbid=146, accessed on 7/6/21.
[2] Australian Catholic School 2008, National Catholic Education Commission, pg 27, accessed from:https://www.ncec.catholic.edu.au/resources/publications/catholic-school-statistics/55-australian-catholic-schools-2008/file on 04/06/21.
[3] Australian Catholic School 2019, National Catholic Education Commission, pg 15,
accessed from:
https://www.ncec.catholic.edu.au/resources/publications/catholic-school-statistics/516-catholic-schools-in-australia-2019/file on 04/06/21.

serious thinking needs to performed to discern approaches for the future.

Rather than despairing about the current situation it is worth looking for signs of hope. Pope Francis has identified one of the roots of the current state of play in respect to the role of parents:

> *...a rift has opened up between the family and society, between the family and school, the educational pact today has been broken; and thus, the educational alliance between society and the family is in crisis because mutual trust has been undermined. ... the number of so-called 'experts' has multiplied, and they have assumed the role of parents in even the most intimate aspects of education.*[4]

This takeover of education by 'experts' has caused mothers and fathers to lose their confidence in their rightful roles. He has encouraged parents to stand up to this power play by experts and reassert their authority:

> *It is time for fathers and mothers to return from their exile — for they have exiled themselves from their children's upbringing — and to fully resume their educational role. I hope that the Lord gives this grace to parents: to not exile themselves from the education of their children. And this can only be done with love, tenderness and patience.*[5]

For Catholic parents to respond to Pope Francis' challenge to return from exile, they need to be prepared to take on an educational role that is more expanded compared to what past generations have had to do. The culture is strongly secular and the strength of traditional institutions such as Catholic schools are not as effective as once they were. Hence the contemporary Catholic parent needs an expanded

---

[4] Pope Francis, General Audience, 20 May 2015 accessed on 7/6/21 from:
https://www.vatican.va/content/francesco/en/audiences/2015/documents/papa-francesco_20150520_udienza-generale.html.
[5] Ibid

vision of their role. Thankfully a theological vision has been developed but is not well appreciated or understood in the broader Catholic Church. This vision started to emerge at the Second Vatican Council held from 1962-65 at around the same time that the entrustment model began to breakdown.

Vatican II and the 'domestic turn'

There are a number of key teachings that flowed out of Vatican II that have a considerable bearing on the issue of the transmission of faith to children that I describe as a '*domestic turn*'. What I mean by this phrase is that there was a reawakening of the role that marriage and family life can play in the Church and society. This reawakening retrieved a way of thinking about the role of the family that had not been enunciated since the patristic era by St Augustine and others.

There were three aspects to this domestic turn that gave new impetus to the Patristic concept. Firstly, there was a renewed understanding of the vocation of the laity[6] and the universal call to holiness[7]. Lay people were called to step out of a passive role and become active agents of evangelisation in their families and workplaces.

Secondly, the theology of the sacrament of marriage was developed substantially. Christian families based on the sacrament of marriage were described as being like domestic churches[8]. Their role was not solely focussed on procreating but they were called to deepen their conjugal love that is enriched by the graces that flow from the sacrament. Hence

---

[6] Vatican II Council, Lumen Gentium, 30-38 accessed on 7/6/21 from:
https://www.vatican.va/archive/hist_councils/ii_vatican_council/documents/vat-ii_const_19641121_lumen-gentium_en.html.
[7] Ibid, 39-42.
[8] Ibid, 11.

spouses have a vocation to love. Their call to parenthood flows from this love.[9]

Thirdly, the call to educate children emanates from the institution of marriage as one of the ends of marriage but also from the conjugal love between the spouses. This teaching is highlighted in the Vatican II document, *Gaudium et Spes*:

> *By their very nature, the institution of matrimony itself and conjugal love are ordained for the procreation and education of children, and find in them their ultimate crown.*[10]

It goes on to add:

> *Authentic married love is caught up into divine love and is governed and enriched by Christ's redeeming power and the saving activity of the Church, so that this love may lead the spouses to God with powerful effect and may aid and strengthen them in sublime office of being a father or a mother.(6) For this reason Christian spouses have a special sacrament by which they are fortified and receive a kind of consecration in the duties and dignity of their state.(7).*[11]

These quotes mentioned above refer to marriage and parenting as a 'sublime office' that also entails a 'kind of consecration' that is caught up in Christ's redeeming love and saving activity.

While this language was promising, the domestic turn didn't become a solid theological reality until the publication of *Familiaris Consortio* in 1981 by Pope St John Paul II following on from the 1980 Synod of Bishops that examined *The Role of The Christian Family in the Modern World*.

---

[9] Vatican II Council, Gaudium et Spes, 48 accessed on 7/6/21 from: https://www.vatican.va/archive/hist_councils/ii_vatican_council/documents/vat-ii_const_19651207_gaudium-et-spes_en.html.
[10] Ibid.
[11] Ibid.

In *Familiaris Consortio*, Pope St John Paul II takes the teaching of Vatican II and extends it further:

> *The sacrament of marriage gives to the educational role the dignity and vocation of being really and truly a 'ministry' of the Church at the service of the building up of her members. So great and splendid is the educational ministry of Christian parents that Saint Thomas [Aquinas] has no hesitation in comparing it with the ministry of priests.*[12]

If the education ministry of parents is comparable to the ministry of an ordained priest then the way that this ministry is respected and incorporated in a broader context of education is very important.

Pope St John Paul II expanded further on the domestic turn in his *Letter to Families* in 1994. I would like to highlight one passage that addressed the close cooperation between the family and the Church when he said:

> *…it is not only a matter of entrusting the Church with the person's religious and moral education, but of promoting the entire process of the person's education 'together with' the Church. The family is called to carry out its task of education in the Church, thus sharing in her life and mission. The Church wishes to carry out her educational mission above all through families who are made capable of undertaking this task by the Sacrament of Matrimony, through the 'grace of state' which follows from it and the specific 'charism' proper to the entire family community.*[13]

---

[12] Pope John Paul II, Familiaris Consortio, 38 accessed on 7/6/21 from: https://www.vatican.va/content/john-paul-ii/en/apost_exhortations/documents/hf_jp-ii_exh_19811122_familiaris-consortio.html.

[13] Pope John Paul II, Letter to Families, 16 accessed on 7/6/21 from: https://www.vatican.va/content/john-paul-ii/en/letters/1994/documents/hf_jp-ii_let_02021994_families.html.

This section of the *Letter to Families* presents a vision of a symbiotic relationship between the Church and the family. The family is called to carry out its task in the Church which it does by virtue of the sacrament of marriage. Concurrently the Church carries out its mission through families.

The manner in which the renewal of Catholic schooling can be achieved will be discussed in Section 3 of this talk. However, it is worth pointing out that the rich development of Church teaching in regards to marriage and parenting that I have described as the domestic turn has not, in the main, been carried over into the guidance documents flowing from the Vatican Congregation for Catholic Education. These documents are used to guide the way Catholic schools are run. Furthermore, the vast majority of discourse in regards to the reform of Catholic education in Australia neglects to incorporate this vision into consideration. Hence the plenary role that parents are called to by the Church and the rich theological vision has not been translated into the structure of the Catholic school system.

Part 2
Our Experience of the Family – School – Church dynamic

So far in this paper I have described some megatrends in relation to the challenge of passing on the faith and have described a renewed theological vision for how the family can be empowered to potentially supercharge this process. I now wish to examine the way the family, parish and the school can play a role in the context of the journey of my own family. The journey has taken place in two states, in three locations and involves experiences of Catholic systems schools, an independent Catholic school, an independent Christian school and a little bit of home-schooling courtesy of the COVID lockdown.

Phase 1
Catholic Education in the Parramatta Diocese from 2011-12

Parish
As a young couple with one child our approach to living our faith was fairly standard as we attended our local parish only 5 minutes' drive from home.

On the birth of our second child we made the move of having her baptised at a parish about 20 minutes' drive across Western Sydney. We began to attend this parish each Sunday. The parish priest was a former spiritual director of mine who gave a fiery sermon and celebrated a reverent Mass that provided spiritual sustenance to a busy young couple. We continued worshipping at this parish for the next 5 years and had our next two children baptised at this parish.

Family
As a family we celebrated baptism days. My wife drove our eldest child to the Catechesis of the Good Shepherd about 40 minutes' drive way. We had a family culture that celebrated Christmas and Easter. Some basic family prayers were said and we didn't celebrate Halloween. We went on some pilgrimages at times of challenge. We also lived in what emerged as a 'Catholic commune' with three other Catholic families moving into the neighbourhood within a few doors of each other. We used to gather monthly for family Rosary celebrations and our children often played together.

School
In terms of education, our children attended the local pre-school and our eldest began school at the local Catholic school.

The school seemed very focussed on discipline. We were the only Smith's at the school. Its student population was 98% Maronite Catholic but only a handful attended the local parish. A large Maronite parish was located a 10-minute drive away.

When the school taught about Halloween and the Christmas concert seemed a bit superficial we began to wonder if this was the best path for our children. We explored other options for education when our eldest child was in Year 1.

We attended an interview with the Principal of Montgrove College, a Pared School on the outskirts of Sydney. The first question she asked us was what virtues we wanted our children to acquire. This question was a breath of fresh air but at the same time very challenging. However, it was the catalyst for our family enrolling our two eldest in the school for 2013 and making the move 30km west to the outskirts of the Sydney Metropolitan area.

Phase 2
Montgrove College – A Pared School from 2013-2017

School

Montgrove College was run differently from a systemic Catholic school. A majority of the children enrolled in the school were from families that regularly practiced the faith. There was a Chapel on campus in which daily Mass was celebrated and regular confession times were scheduled that both students and parents could attend. The school chaplain attended the school a few days a week.

Each family was able to attend a meeting every term with a school tutor who would provide parents with some insight into the personal, spiritual and intellectual development of each of their children. They would also provide some mentoring for the parents on how to raise good children.

Each term a parent night was held for parent formation that was addressed by various experts on parenting. They provided practical input on topics such as how to talk to your kids about puberty and sex education.

There were regular class picnics allowing parents and children to meet each other. When a family had a new baby, the class parents would develop a roster for other families in the class to cook a meal for the family during first few weeks of the baby's life.

They also ran a series of parenting courses for parents with kids in different age groups and it even ran a marriage enrichment program in association with other affiliated schools.

While it was good getting all this input and socialisation we did struggle to find time for doing things as a family unit on top of all the other obligations we had to our extended families.

Parish

We 'parish-shopped' during the first year of our shift west. We found a good parish that was attended by a number of families from the school. The parish priest was very solid and the programs run in the parish were leading edge compared to the other parishes in the area. We had sermons on the nature of traditional marriage while the issue was topical in the media.

Family

As our family began to grow we continued to regularly celebrate feast days for the children's patron saint and also their baptism day using their candles. One year we invited our next-door neighbours to our house for an Easter Sunday Dawn service.

However, as we were at a good school and parish we didn't feel the need to provide too much extra.

A new job opportunity called us away to Hobart.

Phase 3
Catholic Education Tasmania from 2017-18

School

The move to Hobart was a bit challenging as we needed to find a school that could accommodate 4 children to start at the beginning of term 3. We took a trip to Hobart and we had two days to visit some schools and some rental houses to decide on a school and a home.

After a few weeks of Term 3, the marriage plebiscite was called. Some of our kids had arguments about the plebiscite with other kids and they felt that they were in the minority by supporting the No vote.

It became clear that the school was not on the same faith wavelength. There were also some discipline issues and an IT policy that we didn't like.

Parish

We found a good parish at St Mary's Cathedral. We attended Sunday Mass. We got onto the Church cleaning roster and took the whole family to perform this duty. Our eldest two children participated in a Confirmation preparation program. We also participated in the annual Corpus Christi March and a Diocesan event for families.

Family

At home we continued our faith practices. We also supplemented our eldest children's Confirmation preparation at home with an American program. We struggled with the challenge of properly monitor the 3 iPad that came into our house as part of the school.

We fostered our eldest daughter's interest in classical piano that also started to move into literature as well. We bought books on history for the children that they took a liking to.

Phase 4
Calvin Christian School – Christian Schools Tasmania 2019-21

School

At the end of 2018 we decided to move our children to another school as a number of them voiced their concerns. In the beginning of 2019 we sent five of our children to the Calvin Christian school that is run by Christian Schools Tasmania. As part of the enrolment process we were required to sign a form that included a statement of faith that informed us what the school stood for and that we accepted that the school would run according to this statement. While it was based on Protestant theology we agreed with 95% and thought that we would handle the remaining 5% ourselves at home.

We were impressed that the teachers and a number of the families were regular Christian worshippers and this was evident in the practice of prayers and devotions in the school. There were even some practicing Catholics students in attendance.

Our children have been given a good grounding in salvation history through various bible stories. They have encountered some misunderstanding in regards to Catholicism but that happens in any school these days. We have been able to address these issues.

The school communicates well with the parents and they have teacher – parent meetings once a term and a beginning of the year information night/family BBQ for both junior and senior school. The IT policy was stricter than the Catholic Education Tasmania policy and we have been able to manage access to devices with less stress.

The logo of Christian Schools Tasmania is composed of three intertwined strand of a rope that also form a cross. The three strands represent the role that the family, the church community and the school play in educating children. We have felt that the logic of this logo has been put into practice consistent with the statement of faith.

Parish

In terms of our parish at St Mary's Cathedral, our eldest son started to be an altar server in 2019 at the High Mass every week. Our eldest daughter began an organ scholarship and became part of the Cathedral choir. At the beginning of 2019, a Sunday school began and my wife and I got involved as teachers and three of our children attended as well. Unfortunately, the lockdown ensured that this activity was discontinued and it hasn't resumed again since.

Family

At home we continued our family traditions but we also provided some direction to our children to give them a

Catholic perspective on Sacred Scripture and give them some context for the Reformation and the beliefs of non-Catholic Christians. We have introduced our third and fourth eldest children to the Relationship education program that I began with our two eldest children when they were aged 9/10 while they attended Montgrove College. We provide the Catholic context to human sexuality and relationships.

Part 3

Our experience of raising 6 children in a post Christian culture provides a microcosm to review the issue of passing on the faith. The three elements of family, Church and school have been reviewed.

What we have found is that this triple play of elements has worked best when our children attended independent schools. These schools had a strong connection between the parents and the school. We have shared more in common with the families that were attracted to these schools in terms of sharing a focus on faith and the development of character in our children on top of ensuring their sound intellectual development.

The parent formation delivered at Montgrove College was unique and top quality. However, this school and is run by the PARED Foundation that is closely associated with Opus Dei, one of the lay movements within the Catholic Church. It remains to be seen how a school of this nature could be run by a group of Tasmanian parents who were not part of the same lay movement. However, the example of Christian Schools Tasmania (that is part of Christian Schools Australia) shows that it can be possible in the context of Tasmania and other parts of Australia to run an independent school system that is more overt in its Christian emphasis.

Choosing a good parish also helped so that we were both spiritually nourished and our children could see other young people and families in attendance. However, it is rare to come across a parish that provides a lot of help to families to understand the importance of the domestic church.

The Driving Faith Home[14] initiative from the USA is building a movement of protestant churches that are trying to build strong domestic churches. They are encouraging:

- the development of strong marriages via enrichment,
- parents to lead their families spiritually
- make the family home a place of evangelisation to the broader community.

This program is far from widespread but it is producing some good electronic and physical resources for families.

The importance of marriage enrichment that the Drive Home Faith program highlights is very important in relation to the Catholic notion of the Domestic Church. An essential element of the theological vision discussed in Part 1 was that parenting was an overflow of the spousal love of the couple. The development of good marriages, in which conjugal love thrives, is a critical witness for children. When that love overflows into parenting that is authoritative but tender and loving the personal and spiritual development of the children is maximised.

In the current context the only way to reach most Catholic couples is via a school as most do not regularly attend a parish. It remains to be seen whether a systemic Catholic school has the expertise and access to a critical mass of mentor couples to embark on such an exercise. But an independent Catholic school run by parents who are serious about witnessing to the sacrament of marriage may be better positioned to add this important apostolate to its mission.

---

[14] https://www.drivefaithhome.com/.

TASTING THE TRANSCENDENTALS

Robert Van Gend

I was privileged to teach philosophy for four years at Augustine Academy, a small institution that offers a Certificate IV in the Liberal Arts over one year to bridge students into university and other paths. Augustine Academy was founded by Ben McCabe and me in 2016. For the first four years it rented a big house on a 40-acre rural property in Picton, south of Sydney. It is now established on its own land near Tumut. We had between 16 and 23 students each year, with an average age of 17 and a mixture of Christian backgrounds and schooling backgrounds.

We followed the classical liberal arts curriculum quite closely: we offered the Trivium of grammar, logic, rhetoric, as well as three of the Quadrivium of arithmetic, geometry and music. The fourth Quadrivium subject, astronomy, was not a formal study but was covered informally with stargazing nights. Additionally, we introduced students to philosophy, theology, literature, history, debating, science and agriculture.

At the beginning of each academic year, I gave an introduction to the liberal arts to the new cohort. I told them that this year is going to seem useless in the eyes of many; people will likely ask, with a concerned look, 'What kind of job does the liberal arts get you?' C.S. Lewis has the wise answer: 'Friendship is unnecessary, like philosophy, like art ... It has no survival value; rather it is one of those things which give value to survival.'[1] A student of the liberal arts walks with the greatest figures of the Western Tradition, getting to know the best thoughts, imaginative insights, and heroic actions that elevate the human spirit beyond the ordinary world of survival.

I learned at Campion College that in order to appreciate these treasures it is first necessary that one is awoken to wonder, from which comes the desire to know and love truth. Wonder requires stepping back from ordinary survival for a moment, to be astonished by the reality that we take for granted. For instance, when I look at the stars, they provoke the ultimate wondering question: why is there *being* at all? If a society forgets to ask these kinds of questions, if it only asks how to manufacture this car most efficiently or to measure the blood pressure most accurately, it will begin to forget what we are: creatures capable of transcending the everyday world of survival to know and love truth, beauty and goodness and the Persons at the origin of it all.

The pursuit of reality and truth depend on first experiencing wonder, because to wonder is to be awake to reality. Plato described wonder as being taken out of yourself with the desire to know reality. Aristotle said philosophy (the love of wisdom) begins with wonder.

We wanted Augustine Academy to awaken wonder, to draw out the natural desire to know reality that can be muted by so many worldly distractions. Of course, the great texts that we study are sources of wonder, but we wanted this to be enriched by the experience of wonder at creation through hikes in forests and gorges, canoeing adventures and a rural campus of beauty and quiet where the stars are bright and where creation could be discovered and contemplated. The goal was to make Augustine Academy a place to improve in the practice of wonder, to be attentive to the things one normally does not notice. To further this goal, we removed distractions that would prevent the students immersing

---

[1] Lewis, C.S., *The Four Loves*, (New York: HarperCollins, 2002), p.71.

themselves. For instance, students had their phones taken from them upon arrival, and Wi-Fi was only turned on during designated study times.

St Augustine said that we are made with a desire for God, for goodness, truth and beauty. Mainstream culture tells young people that the answer to these spiritual desires is the false food of Netflix binges, excessive alcohol, shallow music, and having all the latest stuff. Not much has changed since St Augustine or the Prodigal Son. At Augustine Academy we wanted to show the students that God, the source of the transcendentals, is the proper answer to our spiritual desires. We hoped to form an alternative culture where students could receive the unforgettable *taste* of the transcendentals, of reality, of their faith and of God. If the excitement of the atheistic mainstream culture is ultimately empty, the excitement of the truth needs to be made as attractive as it actually is.

How did this *tasting* occur at Augustine Academy? For the first four years it operated three days per week with most students residing on campus on the two nights. The residential component meant that there was a lot of time outside of class to create a community life. Learning flowed into meal times and free time. There were discussions about theological concepts over lunch, chats around the fire, and confrontations with real life moral conundrums from sharing life with other students. There was communal prayer in the morning and evening and there were 'read alouds' of books like *The Screwtape Letters* and *The Hobbit*, for leisure, not for study. Students were involved with cooking meals, milking the cow, cultivating soil and growing vegetables for meals, dispatching poultry for dinner, farm maintenance, fence repairs, bread baking, mulberry jam making, meat smoking, candle making and felt making. Some carpentry skills were learned in the construction of a hobbit hole in the side of the hill. Everyone pitched in to make mud bricks from our own clay soil for building a chapel. There were regular lunchtime volleyball matches and games of soccer in the afternoon. The lack of phones and devices to distract them meant they had to work at entertaining themselves in free time. Some took up new instruments or practiced swing dancing for the competition with Campion College. Talent nights, poetry recitations and fireside songs became regular traditions. There was a competitive cook-off in which the girls cooked for the boys one night and the boys for the girls the week after. The staff declared the winner. Each cohort prepared a play or musical (such as *Twelfth Night*, *Pride & Prejudice*, *Peter Pan* and *Fiddler on the Roof*) and performed it to family and friends. One year we held the Augustine Academy Markets where students created wares and baked goods to sell to the broader community.

At least one student got over an attachment to video games and threw himself wholeheartedly into all the activities on the farm. It is a testimony to the power of a good culture to cause someone to lose his appetite for false foods.

The same principle of *tasting* applied to the realities explored in the texts and subjects studied. In order to understand such abstractions as 'the natural order' or the 'Tao' when exploring C.S. Lewis' book *The Abolition of Man*, some firsthand experience of the natural order of things is necessary. Students raised and killed chickens, pigs and sheep, collected the eggs and milked the cow. We thought it was good for the soul and the body to light fires in the winter and swim in the river in the summer, rather than resort to air conditioners all the time. The magnificent sunsets and tranquil sunrises put flesh on the psalmist's insight in the office of morning prayer: 'I rise before dawn and cry for help; I have put my hope in your word.'[2]

In a word, Augustine Academy's philosophy of education is holistic: mind, heart, will, emotions and habits all formed together in a community of faith and learning. By tending to the soil of culture, our aim is to cultivate young people who

---

[2] Psalm 119:147.

desire truth, recognise beauty, discern the good. That, we believe, is a fertile soil in which the faith can put down deep roots.

During 2019, my last year at Augustine Academy, I discovered a book about John Senior, a classics professor at Kansas University who 50 years ago established the Integrated Humanities Program (IHP) with much the same vision as Augustine Academy. In its heyday it attracted over 100 students a year, who were drawn to the unique teaching style of Senior and his associates. In various writings Senior explains his philosophy of education, which was more a recovery of old wisdom than anything original. It could best be described as a *Restoration of Realism*, which is the title given to a book written by Father Francis Bethel, one of the students whose life was changed by Senior.

Senior founded IHP at Kansas University in 1970 with two like-minded professors. To understand the goal of this education project, it is helpful to begin with the problem as Senior saw it. He writes: 'The facts of Christianity are not real to us because nothing is real to us. We have come to doubt the very existence of reality.'[3] How did we get to this place? Senior, who was himself converted to realism by the thought of Thomas Aquinas, agreed with Aquinas that the senses and the intellect collaborate in knowing reality. However, partly due to the success of the new scientific method of measurement and quantification of nature, the Renaissance saw a split between the senses and the reason, pitting them against each other as sources of knowledge. Senior writes:

> The [Rationalists] believed that significance derived from reason. The Romantics attacked them, declaring that significance derived from affections. Modernists attacked them both, repudiating both reason and affection, repudiating the idea of significance itself.[4]

---

[3] Senior, J. in Bethel, F. *John Senior and the Restoration of Realism* (New Hampshire: Thomas More College Press), p.5.
[4] Ibid., p.90.

Robert Frost describes the Modernist mindset thus: 'A blanker whiteness of benighted snow | With no expression, nothing to express.'[5] Reality means nothing; anything we take it to mean is merely a subjective mental state. The implications are logical: there can be no real significance to being right or wrong, male or female, courageous or cowardly. All categories and distinctions are just labels that say nothing of reality.

Ideas have consequences for culture and the influence of Modernism is visible in education. By the time students reach university, they have been formed to be 'skeptical and doubtful of the true, the good and the beautiful, of *being* itself.'[6] Modern students have turned their backs on reality, so the goal of the IHP was to turn them around again so they could use their own eyes, mind and heart to perceive reality, so it could begin to dawn on them that the good and the beautiful are not relative to them but objective and true. Its brochure stated: '[IHP] should be regarded as ... a course for beginners, who look upon the primary things of the world, as it were, for the first time.'[7] The program's motto was *Nascantur in admiratione* ('Let them be born in wonder').

However, Senior found that in order to turn the minds and hearts of students back to reality, he had to go back to foundations. He writes:

> *College teachers faced with freshmen who hate literature, think their job is somehow to convert them – by cajolery, finding something in a text ... relating to their sick, impoverished wants. But the fault was back in high school where they should have loved Shakespeare. But, the high school teacher found his freshmen coming up from elementary school with no desire to read Shakespeare because they had not first loved Stevenson. And the grade school teacher found his students coming up from home without Mother Goose. And more important still, the love*

---

[5] Frost, R. *Desert Places* (1933).
[6] Bethel, op.cit., p.296.
[7] Ibid.

of literature at any stage supposes love of life – grounded in acute sensation and deep emotion.[8]

Senior saw that converting students to reality would require experiential and emotional reconnection to reality. He followed the lead of the ancient Greeks who placed music and gymnastics before more abstractive subjects like philosophy, mathematics, logic, and science. The purpose of this early stage of education was to develop and refine the imagination and emotions, initiate the student in the moral life and aesthetic taste and awaken the intellect.

Gymnastics was all kinds of physical activity for the ancient Greeks. The aim was to develop strength, coordination, endurance and courage. Senior conceived the role of gymnastics as the exercise of the exterior senses through immediate contact with concrete, natural things. Sensation is the primary mode of learning for a child. Senior wrote that 'children need direct, everyday experience of fields, forests, streams, lakes, oceans, grass, and ground' so that the child discovers reality in its variety and richness.[9] However, when a society is saturated with technology, the result is often a lack of direct contact with God's creation. Senior laments the situation:

> *Generations brought up in centrally heated and air-conditioned homes and schools, going from place to place encapsulated in culturally sealed-off buses, swim in heated, chlorinated pools devoid of current, swirl or tide...*[10]

Senior takes aim especially at television which dulls the interior and exterior senses. Its inherent artificiality weakens the grasp on reality. We might be able to watch nature documentaries on television, but it is necessarily a distortion. Senior writes: 'A sixty foot whale splashing across nineteen

---

[8] Senior, op.cit., p.235.
[9] Ibid., p.155.
[10] Ibid., p.143.

inches of your living-room while you sip your Coca Cola is not reality.'[11] A further problem with television is that 'watching it, we fail to exercise the eye, selecting and focusing detail.'[12] Dull senses lead to dull minds and hearts, 'whereas keen, attentive senses and proper delight in reality stir the soul.'[13] You can imagine his reaction to the miniature televisions that we now have in the palm of our hands, distracting us from looking at artificial things like the concrete footpath, let alone from natural things.

The senses can be trained to be more perceptive, as a chef has a cultivated sense of taste and a musician can hear things that others cannot. According to Senior, every attempt should be made to integrate contact with natural things into one's way of life. This will not be easy, because -

[Modern man's] entire environment compels him to gaze vaguely and listen idly; he is both overwhelmed with too much to see and hear, and deprived of anything genuinely interesting to look at or listen to. His senses are restless and distracted with background music everywhere and images flying by as he rushes about in a vehicle.[14]

Senior left the car at home wherever possible, because the experience of walking puts one in much closer contact with creation than driving.

Training of the exterior senses is best achieved by plenty of contact with nature, with God's creations. One aim of gymnastics is to move the senses to delight in reality. Delight should proceed spontaneously from experiencing God's creation. Senior quotes Shakespeare on this point:

> *When daisies pied and violets blue,*
> *And lady-smocks all silver white,*

---

[11] Ibid., p. 144.
[12] Ibid., p.155.
[13] Ibid., p.154.
[14] Bethel, op.cit., p.155.

*And cuckoo-buds of yellow hue
Do paint the meadows with delight.*[15]

Senior was fond of saying that gymnastics begins in experience and ends in delight, music begins in delight and ends in wonder and philosophy begins in wonder and ends in wisdom.

While gymnastics was for the exterior senses, music was for the interior ones – the memory, imagination and emotions. Music for the Greeks was the broad domain of the nine muses: poetry, song, tragedy, comedy, dance, playing instruments, observation of the stars and history (which was stories of heroes). The goal of the musical education was to order the interior senses, such that one learns the right emotional response to a given reality. Those familiar with the *Abolition of Man* will remember that C.S. Lewis talks about the waterfall *meriting* the word 'sublime' and not 'pretty'.[16] The subjectivist dismisses all such judgements as mere feelings with no objective basis, but for Lewis, Senior and the Greeks, emotions can and should be in tune with reality, if they are trained properly.

What did this musical education look like at IHP? The three professors would collectively conduct a lecture which was conversational in style (Fr Bethel points out that *con – versio* means turning together, in this case towards something beautiful and wonderful). They did not speak from notes but led a discussion about the text for the class, being guided by questions from the students. They did not do much theoretical exposition but preferred to use stories and examples to open students' eyes to beauty, to goodness and to the appreciation of virtues. These professors were passionate about their subject and this lent an infectious power to their classes. The professors, along with the great poets and writers since antiquity, taught the students to love

---

[15] Shakespeare, *Love's Labour's Lost*, 5.2.893-6.
[16] Lewis, C.S., *The Abolition of Man* (New York: HarperCollins, 2001), p.2.

reality by tasting it for themselves. These classes opened their hearts to things they had never perceived.

The students had to exercise their musical muscles by memorizing ten poems each semester. They would meet twice a week in small groups and an older student would read a poem aloud. The younger students learned it line-by-line by listening. The IHP brochure stated the reason for this: 'Before attempting to think about poetry, we urge students to simply know and enjoy it as one knows and enjoys any song.'[17] This activity roused their hearts to the beauty of nature, to friendship, fidelity and love. Education under the inspiration of the muses included weekly stargazing sessions, which as Aristotle and Aquinas recognized are a sure path to awakening wonder, the goal of the musical mode.

The principle running through both gymnastic and musical modes of learning was that one must experience something before one can reflect upon it and recognize it. Speaking of a high school situation, Senior writes:

> *In the gymnastic and musical modes, temperance is prefigured in stories, games and the lessons school life teaches in a general way about what is too little and too much ... Against bad habits, the school forms good ones in the daily routine, competitive games, emulation of fictional heroes and the good example of teachers.*[18]

This principle led not only to a good education, but it cultivated a culture. Places like Augustine Academy and IHP owe much of their success to the attractiveness of their culture. Strict prohibitions against getting drunk, sleeping around or playing video games all day will have limited effect on students if they cannot experience for themselves the attractiveness of a life that excludes these things. The heart is restless and will seek the most attractive thing it can find, whether or not it is a truly nourishing thing.

---

[17] Bethel, op.cit., p.299.
[18] Senior, op.cit.., p.255.

As part of the culture-forming experiences at IHP, students took part in activities like learning calligraphy to acquire a taste for doing things beautifully. They were initiated in crafts and ran an old fashioned country fair. There were several formal dances each year, where students 'happily practiced manners, courtesy and grace in the intricacies of the rhythm and steps of the Viennese waltz.'[19] One of the professors remarked of the students' new hobbies: 'Although it would be premature to say that there is a new campus fad of decency, students are beginning to find that barbarism is a bore.'[20] The culture at IHP was attractive, nourishing and exciting, it added legitimacy to the studies, in which the taste of reality was convincing. Students acquired a love of learning, a zest for life and formed lifelong friendships.

Is it a coincidence that in a culture of stargazing, calligraphy, poetry recitations and dancing, dozens of conversions to the faith take place? There were even vocations to the monastery. Unfortunately, this kind of success attracted the attention of powerful figures in the University of Kansas and members of the public who saw the conversions as a sign that IHP was brainwashing students with one view of the world. That was the one view that could not be tolerated. After nine years it was shut down, but its success has spawned many schools in America that are based on Senior's insights.

In summary, the significance of education models like Augustine Academy and IHP is best stated by Senior himself: 'No serious restitution of society or the Church can occur without a return to the first principles, yes, but before principles we must return to the ordinary reality which feeds the first principles.'[21]

---

[19] Bethel, op.cit., p.302.
[20] Ibid.
[21] Senior, op.cit., p.146.

OUR CONTRIBUTORS

Kenneth Crowther is the Head of Secondary at Toowoomba Christian College, where he teaches Literature and Philosophy. He is also a sessional lecturer at the Millis Institute in Brisbane, teaching courses on Literature and Shakespeare. He lives in an off-grid shed on the escarpments of Hampton where he and his wife are slowly introducing their four daughters to the glories of good literature.

Dr David Daintree AM was Principal of Jane Franklin Hall in the University of Tasmania), Rector of St John's College in the University of Sydney, and second President of Campion College Australia (to 2012). He is the founding Director of the Christopher Dawson Centre for Cultural Studies.

Kevin Donnelly AM is a Senior Research Fellow at the Australian Catholic University. Over the last 30 years Kevin has established a reputation as one of Australia's leading conservative commentators and authors fighting against the cultural-left ideology and group think that is poisoning society and stifling free and open debate. Kevin writes for The Australian and the Daily Telegraph and appears regularly on Sky News. His most recent book is titled *Cancel Culture and the Left's Long March* (available at kevindonnelly.com.au). Political correctness denies the ability to reason and be impartial as knowledge, supposedly, is a social construct and all relationships are based on privilege and power. In opposition, Kevin champions the strengths and benefits of Western civilisation, the Enlightenment and our Judeo-Christian heritage that underpin our political and legal systems and way of life and that are being undermined by a rainbow alliance of neo-Marxist, postmodern theories. Kevin was a secondary school teacher for 18 years and in 2014 he co-chaired the review of the Australian National Curriculum. In 2016 Kevin was made a Member of the Order of Australia for services to education.

Fadi Elbarbar was Head of Secondary Religious Education at Sacred Heart College, New Town, 2018 – 2020. Previously he worked for 9 years at St Monica's College, in Epping, Melbourne, where he was the inaugural Coordinator of Social Justice and Service Learning, which saw his initial social justice group 'Be More' grow from 4 students, to 200 students, plus 150 alumni. That social justice program at SMC was considered a benchmark for similar programs. Fadi has a Masters of Educational Leadership from Melbourne University is completing his Masters of Theology at BBI-TAITE. He is currently the Learning Area Leader for Religious Education at Parade College in Melbourne. In 2021, Fadi co-founded 3 Steps Away, a startup focussing on using the See, Judge, Act model to promote active citizenship to secondary students.

Dr Gerard Gaskin has worked in four different Catholic Arch/dioceses and has held senior leadership roles at school principal, Assistant Director and Director levels. He has been deeply involved in seminary formation and his academic qualifications include a Masters thesis that synthesises a pedagogical theory derived from the Ancient Greeks by the Medieval scholars, as well as successful Doctoral thesis in Catholic educational leadership. He has written numerous curriculum documents and educational articles, and presently assists with PhD candidate supervision and examination. His current role is Executive Director of Catholic Education in Tasmania.

Dr David Hastie is Associate Dean, Education Development, at Alphacrucis College. Previously he was Education Strategist for the Anglican Schools Corporation (ASC. David is committed to strategically growing Australian student outcomes across multiple schools, school systems and tertiary sectors, by enhancing learning outcomes and school culture. He is a Committee Member of the NSW Institute for Education research, has published and presented extensively at education conferences. He has also written numerous policy and Parliamentary submissions, most recently responses to the Senate Legal and Constitutional Affairs References Committee's inquiry into legislative exemptions that allow faith-based educational institutions to discriminate against students, teachers and staff; the response to the National Regional, Rural and Remote Education Strategy (NRRRES); and the House of Representatives standing committee on Employment, Education and Training's inquiry into the status of the teaching profession.

Cheryl Lacey is a Melbourne-based parent, author and advocate for education. As a 'navigator of the educational landscape', she investigates landmark policies and practices and suggests directions for change. She works with parents, and professional educators, calling on them to make their voices heard in education-related discussions and essential reform.

Eamonn Pollard began his teaching career as a Religious Education specialist at Guilford Young College in 1998. He has degrees specialising in Accounting, History, Religious Education and Theology and is a candidate for a PhD at the University of Tasmania. The topic of his PhD is the relationship between service learning and teenager eudaimonia (flourishing). Eamonn is presently Principal of St Aloysius Catholic College. When his youngest child turns 13 this July he will be father to four teenagers who give him a daily education on what it means to be a teenager.

The Most Revd Dr Julian Porteous was ordained a priest for the Archdiocese of Sydney on 7th September, 1974. In 2002 he was appointed Rector of the Seminary of the Good Shepherd, Sydney and served in this role until the end of 2008. Pope John Paul II named him Auxiliary Bishop of Sydney in July 2003, and Pope Francis appointed him to be the eleventh Archbishop of Hobart in 2013. Archbishop Porteous is actively involved in evangelisation, particularly among young people. He promotes the role and work of the new ecclesial movements as a grace given to the Church in our time to renew the Catholic faith and promote the evangelising mission of the Church. Archbishop Porteous chose as his motto, *Gratia et Veritas* ('Grace and Truth'), a reference to John 1:17. Archbishop Porteous has published widely: his most recent book is *Foundations: Preparing the Church in Australia for the Plenary Council and Beyond*.

The Revd Peter Robinson is an ordained minister of the Anglican Diocese of Sydney. He studied for ordination at Cambridge (where he met David Daintree) and at Ridley College Melbourne. With an English/History teaching background in NSW state schools Peter's parish incumbencies both included active involvement in local state school SRE teaching or governance. His key commitments until 2008 have been to the parish and the role of the whole people of God in the local community, especially through combined churches SRE. As chair of the local SRE board in the Shoalhaven region of NSW which had grown to employ 6 SRE teachers in 4 high schools teaching 2,500 students on an annual budget of over

$300,000 he was asked in 2008 to become CEO of Generate Ministries, established in 2005 by Anglican Youthworks, Scripture Union, the Baptist Union and Presbyterian Youth to employ NSW state high school SRE teachers on behalf of local combined churches' SRE boards. Employing 250 SRE teachers, school chaplains and staff when he finished at Generate in 2015, today it employs over 400 teachers and chaplains throughout NSW. His interest in the history of SRE in Eastern Australia and the seminal role of Governor Richard Bourke (1831-37) has developed out of this experience.

Ben Smith has worked as the Director of the Office of Life, Marriage and Family at the Archdiocese of Hobart (July 2017 – present) and in the Diocese of Parramatta (June 2014 - June 2017). During this time he has run a number of events and developed a range of faith resources to help families pass on the faith. He has also written extensively and spoken at conferences on the topics of family faith practices.

Julianna Smith graduated from Sydney University in 1999 with an Arts/Law degree. She worked for Freehills in Sydney as a commercial lawyer for 5 years prior to the birth of her eldest child. For the last 15 years she has been a stay at home mother.
Ben and Julianna Smith have been married for 16 years and are the parents of 6 children aged from 4 to 15.

Karl Schmude KSG has combined a career in university librarianship and freelance writing with a co-founder role in the development of Campion College Australia. He has published widely on religion and culture in Australian and overseas journals and produced other works, including short biographies of G.K. Chesterton and Christopher Dawson. He serves as President of the

Australian Chesterton Society and editor of its quarterly newsletter, *The Defendant*.

Dr Wanda Skowronska is an educational psychologist and has worked in several inner Sydney schools as well as counselling for the Catholic organisation Family Life International. She spent her early years in Bonegilla Migrant camp where her parents had come as refugees from Poland and Latvia. She studied at the John Paul II Institute in Melbourne completing a PhD there in 2011, writing on the integration of psychology and Christian anthropology, focusing on the work of American Catholic psychologist Paul Vitz. She did several years of sessional lecturing at the John Paul II Institute. She has written articles for several journals, and was a regular contributor on psychological matters and cultural change for the Australian Catholic journal *Annals*. She has written a book on the experiences of post-World War II refugees entitled *To Bonegilla from Somewhere* (2013), *Catholic Converts from Down Under ... And All Over* (2015) a book on Catholic education, *Angels Incense and Revolution: Catholic Schooldays of the 1960s* (2017), and more recently *Fr Paul Stenhouse: A Life of Wisdom, Compassion and Inspiration* (2020).

Robert van Gend graduated from Campion College, Sydney in 2014 with the College Medal for the Bachelor of Arts in the Liberal Arts. He was awarded an unconditional pass for his Masters thesis on the reality of the mind at the University of Notre Dame, Sydney. In 2020 he commenced a PhD at Notre Dame on Thomas Aquinas and the intelligibility of nature. Between 2016-2019, Robert served as a founding member, philosophy lecturer and Academic Dean of Augustine Academy in Picton, which offers a Certificate IV in the Liberal Arts in a rural setting to students aged between 16-20.

www.ingramcontent.com/pod-product-compliance
Lightning Source LLC
Chambersburg PA
CBHW050308010526
44107CB00055B/2149